MW00608032

Copyright was under the title:
TWEEK and ME – A STORY OF THE HEART

ISBN: 978-0-578-72597-0

FOR ALL IS LOVE

A SPIRITUAL JOURNEY OF ETERNAL LOVE

Twin Souls: The Woman On The Other Side, The Man On This Side And Their Extraordinary Story Of Determination To Be Together

FELECIA (KLEA) and
LEN (URA) LA SCOLEA

DEDICATION

Klea and Ura dedicate this book to all the souls on this Earth who made the courageous decision as eternal spirit beings to take on human form to learn about love. Love being the total essence of the Soul. There is great truth in that love truly does conquer all.

A Heart Felt Thank You to Rosemary, David, Tony, Laura, Vicki and Jamie.

ACROSS THE TRAVAILS OF TIME WE HAD MANY NAMES, GUISES, AND FACES, THROUGH MANY BATTLES, TRIALS, AND TRIBULATIONS. HOWEVER, THROUGH THE AGES ACROSS TIME AND SPACE, IT WAS US, STILL US.

KLEA AND URA

OUR ETERNAL SPIRIT NAMES

OUR REAL NAMES

LETTER TO THE SKEPTIC

The definition of the skeptic is a "disbeliever." The first question one must ask is what do you base this disbelief on? I cannot overemphasize the fact that I was the ultimate skeptic based on my background. So what made me make a dramatic change? After all faith and belief work for others but not for me. My position can be summed up in two words, "overwhelming evidence." The evidence had better be impeccable to support the facts. Always follow the evidence wherever it may take you. The evidence may make you uncomfortable, but the fact remains, what is the evidence telling a rationale, objective, analytical mind? Remember we have a massive degree of evidence in the last 170 years, especially the last 40 years, from many different medical and scientific disciplines as outlined in this book. This evidence and information would fill vast rooms. There is so much evidence that there is no need to hope within our hearts anymore of a life after this life. It is a fact! Keep in mind no one, I mean no one, has ever come close to proving there is not life before and after this life, ever! When one examines the totality of evidence in numerous medical and scientific circles you come away with there is no doubt to a rational mind.

This is about truth. A truth that is both liberating and empowering. Free yourself of being a prisoner of a belief system.

Let us take you to that place of remembering deep within you and your consciousness. Let us all have the courage to investigate and see where the evidence takes us. This book is for you too. This is an invitation to you to make you aware of some of this voluminous proof. In chapter 20, I devoted a complete chapter to you. This is all our story, if you truly believe in the power of love. So come with us. Open your mind. Depart from your comfort zone. This truth will certainly set you free. Depart from your belief system and join us on a journey of eternal love across time and space.

Contents

Prologue

This story has no end, because love is forever. Love is eternal. Love will never die. This is a love story. A story of the heart across dimensions. A story across time and space. This is a human story. This is a spiritual story. This is not a ghost story. This is a story of nonfiction. The heart is for love, truth and knowing. The heart is the bridge between human and spirit. This is about the true heart. Love is the most powerful energy in our entire spiritual universe. Love is always the answer. Long ago our souls mated as one. This story began sometime in the stone age with the inception of our two souls then through the many thousands of years. Her timeless great love motivated me to write this book. It would have been impossible for me to write this book without her. From The Other Side, the Spirit World, she told and taught me so much. This story was written for you the reader. This story was written for all of us. Those who truly understand the power and the wonderment of love, so that you will realize we are so much more than flesh and blood. This story reveals where we came from, our true HOME called The Other Side. Why we are here? And of the return to our true HOME. Earth being our home away from HOME. This story is about all of us. This story is about who and what we really are. We are more than flesh, we are love. Life never ends. Consciousness, the total awareness of everything, is eternal. Love never ends. There is order and no coincidences in everything in this spiritual universe. This story is about our souls. This is a story about love and the soul , the eternal enduring powerful essence of who we really are. So come with us on our journey of love across time and space.

CHAPTER 1

THE BEGINNING

In my wildest dreams I never thought I would be writing a book of this nature. If you would have said to me years ago I would be writing a book like this, my response would have been "Are you nuts?" "Just put a net over my head and take me away!" This is a true story. Every event actually happened down to every detail. This was not in my imagination or wishful thinking; none of that nonsense. I am a no nonsense guy. I was the ultimate skeptic. This is our story. This story must be told. This book is for all of us who believe in the power of love. There is NOTHING that love cannot conquer. To understand the heart of any story you have to return to the beginning.

I was conceived the same month the Atomic Bomb was born. I grew up in the first year of the baby boom generation in 1946, just after World War II. It was Ashes to Ashes; Dust to Dust back then. Life before and after this Life on this Earth was total nonsense. Growing up in the Bronx, New York in a hard environment there was no room for imagination, intuition, the spirit and spiritualism, meditations, psychic thoughts, just the hard knocks of life in this existence. The school of thought was to believe nothing of what you hear and half of what you see. FUHGEDDABOUTIT! As they say New York Tough or Bronx Tough. Furthermore, being raised as a Roman Catholic boy in an Italian family with pictures of the Blessed Mother, the Crucifix and Jesus around the house, the beginning and end was the teachings of the Roman Catholic Church. You know go to Mass every Sunday, Heaven and Hell, you are born then you die, you are here just once, the devil vs. God; follow the rules and if not, you end up in Hell for eternity, not eating meat on Friday, obligated to go to church on Sunday, doing penance as punishment for sins, the whole confession and communion thing, required to confess your sins to God, if not punishment is waiting, then recite an Act of Contrition, to get our sins forgiven and of course on Good Friday at Easter total silence and reflection in the afternoon and on it goes. My family and it was a large one with all the grandparents, aunts, uncles and all the degrees of cousins followed all these tenets of the Catholic Church because everyone wants to get into Heaven and certainly not go to Hell, and be with the red being with the horns and his buddies, right?

This was my mindset for many years of my early life. A thought of a Life before and after this Life was not in the cards of thinking. I was the ultimate skeptic, especially spending my complete life in medicine and science. IF THERE WAS ANY ONE MORE SKEPTICAL THAN ME, I WOULD LIKE TO MEET THAT PERSON. Almost everything can be explained by these disciplines of medicine and science; right? Everything was this material world in front of us detected by our very crude five senses. If you could not see it, taste it, touch it, smell it, and hear it, it simply did not exist. Now let us fast forward to the best day of my life, Saturday, September 24, 1977. This life anyway, I cannot speak for my other numerous past lives, which is a story later in this book. The day I and Tweek were married. Her nickname was Tweek because one night when we were dating in the 1970's she got in the car and I looked over at her and it just "popped" into my head, Tweek, a beautiful, sweet, gentle little bird. We even had baby blue T-Shirts made up with Tweek on one and Baby on the other. Throughout our home were the two birds in pictures and rugs. My nickname she called me was Baby. So there you go!

Now for the worst, most horrible day of this life on Monday, November 5, 2018 at 5:31 in the early morning, she was there at 5:30 and one minute later she was gone. You see, she had lung cancer but never smoked a day in her life. After a 15 month battle with this terrible form of cancer where she had some of the best therapy available, my Felecia, my heart, died in my arms in our kitchen. She was the most courageous person I have ever known, strong, brave and true to the last moment. I did not know it then, this would be the beginning of our Spiritual Journey of love and the heart. The heart will never ever be denied. The heart is for knowing, truth and most of all for love. The heart will always set things right in your being.

CHAPTER 2

THE AFTERMATH OF HER DEATH

After the initial numbness and shock within the mind, one simply does not think normally from such grief and trauma. In addition, there was great guilt of being in the medicine and science profession and not being able to save her. My heart was in a million pieces never to heal. Why bother to open my eyes in the morning? There was no life without her. Each passing day was a struggle to survive. Each day you cry a little bit, you bleed a little bit and you die a little bit. She gave me purpose. She gave me peace. My Felecia was the reason to be strong. She gave me strength and power. Doing normal daily activities became an insurmountable task of epic proportions. For instance, two weeks after her passing I am sitting in our dining room attempting to do the finances of the household. I sat there for a good 20 minutes looking at a blank check I was to fill out. It was like my mind and body were in a state of paralysis. I simply did not care about anything or anyone. The outside world did not exist for me anymore, and still today most of the outside world is frivolous nonsense now. I totally shut out the world. I literally walked around in a total daze, like a zombie in the movies. It was like a living death. I would ask why do I still wake up in the morning? Why do my eyes still open? What is the point? Eating was no longer a joy it was to keep on living now to eat food. We used to enjoy Happy Hour every day now there is no longer any hour of happiness.

This is a dramatic transformation because both of us being Italian; great food especially Italian Cuisine was one of the reasons for existence. Great Italian food was a religion. In general, any great food and drink was a religion. My Tweek, my heart, was an incredible Italian cook with much love in the preparation of the food. She would go into the kitchen and create magic out of nothing many times. I would numerous times have to catch an early morning flight for work and she would be making me breakfast at 4:00 AM in the morning. This alone says what a beautiful soul she was. At parties I use to introduce us as, "OK she is a much better person than me so let us just move on now." My girl was so giving and loving. There was not a selfish, me first, instant gratification, bone in her beautiful body. My Tweek took care of the family in so many loving, unselfish and giving ways. She was the nucleus of the family. The family revolved around her unconditional love. She made us all better than what we were. Felecia was the finest human being I ever knew. Tweek was the family. My girl was simply the best of the best.

Our marriage was not like many where a couple stays together for money, habit, convenience, the children, family obligation, many times a couple will hate each other, and other reasons which have nothing to do with love. There are so many marriages out there devoid of love. I noticed that many people I know don't have a clue about a marriage of deep love. I feel very sorry for them. They are missing so much. Although we had a large family, happiness was my girl and me. Love is the true essence of life.

Of course everyone has their ups and downs over long periods of time. Who doesn't? Did I act like a "jerk", a fool, make big mistakes at times? Absolutely, yes! However, I say anyone who did NOT act like a fool, make mistakes or be a "jerk" then please cast the first stone. "Judge not lest you be judged." Then that individual is truly perfection. That is what it is all about in this life, Love with a Big L and La Famiglia. All of that other stuff we worry about, when it comes down to it, is such trivial nonsense, a distraction from what is really important. It takes a tragedy like this to wake you up. This "wake up call" is permanent and you never forget.

So what was my life like in the aftermath of her passing away? In a word, a total "nightmare," no ending and stays with you every moment of your existence. It is relentless pain. She gave meaning to everything. Every day was anguish of the heart, pain and suffering with no relief. Why should I take my next breath? Forget about getting out of bed. To use a Bronx analogy it is like getting "beat up" with a baseball bat not only physically, but also mentally, emotionally and spiritually 24/7. I totally imploded. You are totally off balance in every aspect of your being. I didn't even know who I was any more. Your whole soul, your very being is in devastation mode.

Many days you simply don't get out of bed. Grief has you down for the count. I truly understand what a broken heart is now. I could now understand how a person could die of a broken heart. You cry and die a little bit each day, every day. I knew, I would never be complete again nor healed until I made the transition to join her. I would never have peace again till we were reunited. She was, and is, my heart for all eternity. One cannot live without a heart. I did not sleep in our bedroom for many months. I slept on the family room couch, very close to her recliner chair that she slept in when she got sick. The upheaval of our lives began with the lung cancer diagnosis. I was on a mission to cure her. If she had needed anything during the night, I was right there to get it for her: medicines, tea, whatever my girl needed. I never wanted her to feel she was ever alone. For this fifteen-month cancer nightmare I never left her side for one moment.

Many times each day I would pull up to her chair and sit on a low small bench to be very close to her and just hold her hand to let her always know she was never alone. It is beyond agony to see the person who is your heart suffer so much. It was fifteen months of intense trials and tribulations. Dominating your life, your very existence. A never- ending parade of doctor appointments, all forms of therapies, and diagnostic scans. Anything else in life simply gets pushed aside and becomes unimportant. There was one focus, HER.

Three weeks after her passing away, I attended Hospice of Buffalo, New York grief counseling sessions. These are wonderful people who do a very much-needed service for people in all stages of grief. A group of people sitting in a room, and then by taking turns, start to tell their tragic story. It is a heart breaking experience to witness all the deep pain and suffering of people. So many tears; I never cried so much in my entire life following her passing away. You could have filled an ocean with tears. When it came to my turn, I described the long 15 month medical history battle with a very difficult form of lung cancer, until that fateful morning on November 5, 2018. I described what we meant to each other for 43 years. Where we did everything together, like two birds in a cage. Now one bird is gone, what happens to the other bird? You simply don't wash away 43 years. Where one began and the other ended you could not tell. At times we felt "Twin Like." Unknown to my conscious mind this was closer to the truth than I could ever imagine. I told the children during this period of extreme agony that half of me was gone. You should have buried me in the ground with her. I knew then that I would never recover from a devastation of this magnitude. I truly understand the constant anguish of the heart. The shock was too great. I never could conceive, nor accept, that my girl would actually die. I had no interest in life any more. My hope was always the next therapy. Near the end she started to turn down various therapeutic options. She knew and accepted the reality of which I simply could not. Even to this day, at times, I am still in shock and numb of what happened. I believe I will never fully accept the fact of her passing away; at the age of sixty-six, which is not old in this day and age. I will never recover. Maybe God takes all his angels early. I don't know what I was, in hell, very angry with God! Yes, there are greater tragedies but this was our tragedy. Ten days from her sixty-seventh birthday on November 15th. You always ask yourself why does something so horrible happen to such a loving, kind, compassionate person? Someone who is love itself. Then you have the "dirtbags" of the world, where nothing ever happens to them. If you try to create a logical reason for a person so loving contracting and suffering from a terrible disease you simply would lose your mind and get lost in the what "ifs" and what "nots."

The group I was associated with at the Hospice Center were amazed that after just three weeks I was attending their meetings. I was totally lost, I needed somewhere to go and to just talk to people who were experiencing deep grief as I was. After a while I stopped going to the Hospice meetings because of all the repetition and the same things said over and over again, that all this takes time for the beginning of the healing process. However, I knew from the beginning of this tragedy I would never ever recover from this, no matter how long the journey of time. A wound of the heart like this is so deep it never heals.

The depth of pain is so great I could not even find a bottom to it. The vacuum of loss was so great I could not comprehend it. I simply could not get my mind around it. All the talking, counseling in the world are just words. Her importance to the family and me was beyond any word description. A person enters the dark depths of despair. I was in a very dark place. At times this is called "The Dark Night of the Soul." My Soul; my very being was damaged beyond repair. Then in the dark depths of despair your mind starts to think of joining her by putting an end to yourself.

Thoughts were present to put an end to this constant never ending deep pain. At times these feelings of suicide become so strong you start to plan how you are going to execute (no pun intended) the plan for your final moments here in this physical rotten world. One's thoughts go to a very quick method with minimal pain. However, then you start to think you have children and grandchildren; the effect on them would be devastating that Dad/Papa committed suicide. So you stay alive in this miserable rotten agony for another day and the day after and the one after that. The eternal anguish and suffering of the heart goes on.

At these Hospice meetings, the people talked about how there were numerous signs and "feelings" that their loved ones were still with and around them. At first my thoughts were these people are so grief stricken that they are comforting, "feel good" thoughts and imagination. These people are talking about "feelings" and "signs"? I laughed. I am the "facts, evidence guy": the medicine, science, Bronx guy. After several descriptions of experiences of After Death Communication, it piqued my interest enough to start to ask questions. My curiosity got the better of me.

That is when in the midst of conversation it was mentioned that there was a specific woman in Lilydale, NY who was the "real deal" with the gift to communicate with the dead. A Medium is simply a middleman or woman for spirits on The Other Side and us here on This Side called Earth and so we can have a conversation. Now here I am thinking of that movie years ago with the actor Bruce Willis, The Sixth Sense, when the little boy in this movie says "I see dead people." So I say to myself, "self" now you finally lost it! You basically "flipped your lid." A saying when I was a "kid" was "The men in the white coats will be coming for you, to take you away." I said to myself "what the hell?" I've got nothing to lose. Losing her was losing everything anyway. Let's give this a try. I was at a stage to try anything. Subsequently, I decided to pursue a Reading with this woman at Lilydale. This day of the Reading on December 19, 2018 would be the beginning of a long Spiritual Journey that had many unexpected twists and turns with a meeting with destiny.

CHAPTER 3

THE AWAKENING

Now Lilydale, which is about a one-hour drive from Buffalo, New York, is the largest site in the world for Spiritualism. What is Spiritualism? If you look up various definitions of Spiritualism you essentially get this: It is a religion based on the belief that the spirits of the dead exist and have both the ability and inclination to communicate with the living. The Afterlife, or the "Spirit World", is seen by spiritualists, not as a static place, but one in which spirits continue to evolve and communicate with us here.

I called and made an appointment for a Reading at Lilydale with this gifted woman. I will not mention names for two reasons. First, this is a story about Tweek and Me. Secondly, people have the sacred right to have their privacy protected. Now my mindset going into this reading was no expectations and a totally clear mind. I was an open-minded skeptic. The key phrase is "open minded." The only thing this woman knew about me was my first name. I kept my mind totally blank in case this woman could read my mind having psychic ability. All of the information described by this Medium was not in my mind in any way. A prayer was given then the Reading began.

The emotional atmosphere was that things were going downhill the past year or so. Felecia came through immediately loud and clear. The Medium was impressed at how clear and strong she came through. It became apparent Felecia was crushed by her own sudden passing. She was totally surprised. She did not expect this. Felecia was "broadsided." She thought there was more time here in this Earth plane. The Medium stated her sister's name, Kathy, being with her, standing next to her; she passed away years before, as being with Felecia. The Medium was making circling motions over the chest area. She stated there was an illness, not an accident, in her passing; and it was in the chest area but not the heart. This woman explained that spirit "thinks at us", through pictures, symbols, thoughts, various images, words, smells, feelings and this has to be interpreted by the Medium. Felecia showed her our monument at the cemetery and then showed her our wedding rings. What do the wedding rings have to do with the cemetery, she asked? I then proceeded to explain that on the monument we had carved our wedding rings with the date we got married, 9/24/77.

This woman actually talked about our married life, time frames, things that no one else would know. Yes, this woman really started to get my interest. She mentioned that Felecia had cancer and I was getting panic and anxiety attacks. She also mentioned that Felecia's sister Kathy was a baseball jock in her 20's, this was correct and was impossible for her to know.

Felecia was very upset in her passing and had a stream of swear words. She knew that when my girl was sick, I always made her fruit milk shakes in the morning for her nutrition. She described the Salmon Fish hanging on the basement wall from an Alaska trip. The Medium mentioned that I would be going to Florida after Christmas and befriend a man down there. This turned out to be correct.

Felecia had discovered on Facebook long lost relatives in Italy. This Medium talked about it, and the name of the relative in Italy, Marcella. This woman also knew I did not call her many times by her name Felecia but by a "nickname" Tweek, WOW! There were so many other details that she was mentioning about Felecia that were impossible for anyone to know. She said “eleven” keeps coming up, the month of her passing and her birth month, November. Numerous details about our home were described because Felecia was telling her since she is always with me in our home every day. So I sat there in silent total amazement. The key piece of information was that this Medium wanted me to write Felecia a letter every day. Just telling her about my day and all my feelings, emotions. It will be my time with just her.

The woman said that after a while you will start to see a SHIFT. “Things will start to happen.” I left with this take home lesson to start to write her daily letters. I departed impressed and in awe of this Medium because she was correct about so much, that it would be impossible for others to know. My skepticism somewhat started to melt. Little did I know that there was so much more to come, beyond all my wildest dreams and imagination.

CHAPTER 4

THE 2018 HOLIDAY SEASON

As I drove home my mind was very active, curious, and impressed as to what I just experienced with this Medium. There was no way this woman could have known all of these details about Felecia and me, our life together, the last forty three years. I analyzed in my mind all rational options to explain this incredible experience that I just had with this Medium. The only rational explanation was that she was actually in contact in communication with Felecia, my Tweek. In fact, this experience was so powerful, that it was irrational not to accept this conclusion. The ultimate skeptic mindset was starting to have doubts. There appeared to be communication with my Felecia after she had passed away.

The next day, on December 20, 2018 I decided to start to write her a letter every day. I wrote my girl a letter every morning. I talked about what I was going to do that day. I expressed my deep pain, sorrow, grief and the despair of losing her. The pain just poured out of me onto the paper. It was pure anguish beyond anything I had ever experienced. My love for her was beyond any words that could ever be described. Missing her was beyond anything I could ever imagine. My mind, heart, spirit and soul were in deep constant pain.

I expressed every possible human emotion in those letters every day. The Holiday Season was upon us, and it was a total utter nightmare. Christmas had been a very special time of year for us. Decorating our home, and our Christmas tree, was such a joyful time of year. It was filled with so much love, caring, joy and laughter. She made it a home of love. It was a cooking and baking extravaganza, with all kinds of Italian "yummy" dishes. Christmas Eve was The Feast of the Seven Fishes and baking of all kinds of Italian Christmas cookies. My girl was truly amazing. She had such a love and talent for cooking and baking. Everything she made was truly exceptional because she poured so much love into doing it. It was such a wonderful time of year, our favorite time of year with family, friends and much love. Now all of this was gone, lost forever. Nothing was any good anymore. I was simply totally destroyed in every parameter of measurement. Christmas 2018 was spent with my brother Joe who lives near Poughkeepsie, New York. It was just Joe and I, since our Mom and Dad had passed away many years before. It was the worst Christmas of my life. The level of depression was so deep that it was a tangible entity in the air. Nothing was good anymore nor mattered. There was nothing to look forward to. However, I still kept writing those letters every day. Every day was bad to very bad. There was no such thing as a good day. Those days were lost forever. When it was a very bad day I would write two letters in the same day, and a few times three letters in one day. For New Years, how was I going to survive this holiday that looks forward to the next year, 2019? What a joke, being happy about the coming year! I was planning on traveling to Florida in February just to clear out my head.

Early in December I went to AAA and mentioned that I wanted information on Florida because I was going to get away since I was a very recent widower. The woman at AAA said, ohh! You must join our Solo Club for widows, widowers and other singles. In fact this year for New Years they were going to Boston to watch the fireworks on a ship in Boston Harbor. I said to myself, "what do I have to lose" and I was off to Boston for New Years with the AAA Solo Club.

I had a total utter meltdown New Year's Eve and wrote her three letters that day. I returned to my room and everything just hit me. I fell apart.

The people were very nice but nothing could comfort me. I was inconsolable. As the band was playing on the ship I watched the Fireworks in Boston Harbor. As it struck that bewitching hour of midnight ushering in the next year, the emptiness inside was too much to bear. There was a huge hole where my heart was supposed to be. This was the first Christmas and New Year's without her in 43 years. The pain was beyond anything imaginable. It was so deep I could not even begin to comprehend it. The Holiday Season simply was a total disaster. Obviously, our home was not decorated for Christmas, and never will be, ever again. We had extensive Christmas decorations, many with great sentimental value. I was hitting rock bottom in every way possible. I was destroyed in every imaginable way. I would watch happy couples of all ages, and just cringe and bleed inside. Well, the 2018 Holidays were over, thank God.

Now it was early January 2019. The New Year brought in great hope and joy for many, but for me it was just preparing to visit Florida and to make an attempt to clear out my head and heart. It was simply trying to survive one day at a time. I was just passing the hours and days. The only hope I had was to join my girl soon. I was still writing her a letter every day telling her about my activities and constant pain and despair. During the middle of January, things started to happen, as The Medium in Lilydale said that there would be a "SHIFT." The first contact occurred. Well, I kept a diary of the electronic messages I started to receive from my Felecia; which totally surprised me, to no end.

CHAPTER 5

FIRST CONTACT: THE ELECTRONIC MESSAGES

As I continued to write every day to my eternal heart, my Felecia, nothing had happened at first. However, into the middle of January 2019 I was starting to get messages of an electronic nature. In my research, one of the most common forms of After Death Communication (ADC) is that the spirit people use the manipulation of electronics to communicate. Anything electrical can be manipulated: the T.V., lights being turned on and off, radios changing stations and staying 'on' and still playing, while being 'off ' and computers being turned on. Anything electronic can be affected. Now all of a sudden the number 11 seemed to be everywhere. I started to see multiple times 11:11 on my cell phone just by "so called" chance. If there was a clock anywhere in the house 11:11 and 4:44 were appearing all the time now. Then I started to smell, Felecia's, soft mild, beautiful perfume several times, especially when I would wake up in the mornings or go to sleep at night. Sometimes her perfume would be there, even during the night when I was awake in bed, just thinking.

There is a free standing globe light in the family room. Now you have to turn the switch TWICE for this light to go on. It started one evening; this light was turning on, all by itself! To say that I was shocked is an understatement.

One afternoon as I started to pack upstairs for my trip to Florida, leaving on February 1st, an old computer where one has to push down on a large power button and hold it down and then processing through to the home page, started to go on full blast by itself. Who pushed down on the power button of this old computer and held it down to turn it on and then go through the processing to the home page? A CD player in the dining room, which has several functions for iPod, CD and Radio, one day around noon automatically turned to a specific radio station talking about NOT committing suicide. Why automatically turn to that specific station at that particular time to talk about not committing suicide? I did not turn to this radio station. It turned to this station all by itself. I was seeing off-season birds on the front porch and by the kitchen window like Red Cardinals, Blue Jays of which I mentally recorded but which did not mean much to me.

A few days later I was finishing my packing for my Florida trip and all was quiet. However, later in the afternoon, I was going up the stairs and I heard music playing. Now where was this music playing out of nowhere coming from? The music was coming from our bedroom at the far end of the hall. Now I have not slept, nor have gone into our bedroom for several months after she passed away. As I entered our bedroom, the music was coming from an old fashioned clock radio in the corner on Felecia's side of the bed. Now this clock radio has a big slide that you have to push all the way to turn the radio on. It takes a significant effort to turn this radio on. While the radio was totally off and the slide was all the way in the off position, it still was playing. So how the "hell" is this radio playing when off? So how do you turn a radio OFF from playing when it is already OFF? I pulled the plug to cut the power and the radio stopped playing. However, as soon as I plugged it in again it started playing. Later on, when I returned from Florida and plugged it in, it was still playing in the off position. Months later, I plugged this radio in again and it started playing. This radio now eternally plays in the OFF position when you plug it in; I was amazed to say the least.

How our loved ones on The Other Side, that is what it is called, send us After Death Communication (ADC) includes all these forms of electronic messages. They also can communicate by ringing doorbells and no one is there. Pennies appearing out of thin air. These messages with objects appearing out of thin air are called Apports. Other examples are, hearing music and voices when no one is around and several other forms of communication.

At this point I said OK Felecia, you definitely have gotten my attention. "HOW MANY TIMES DOES A GUY HAVE TO GET HIT OVER THE HEAD TO SAY OK SOMETHING IS DEFINITELY GOING ON?" Thus, having been all my life, in medicine and science, doing comprehensive, rigorous, exhaustive research is in my DNA. I now entered the world of The Near Death Experience (NDE) and The After Death Communication (ADC) fields of which I had no knowledge of, and no preconceived ideas.

CHAPTER 6

THE NEAR DEATH EXPERIENCE (NDE) and THE AFTER DEATH COMMUNICATION (ADC) RESEARCH

Felecia truly attracted my curiosity and interest in Life After this Life. I learned through our Spiritual Journey that the term Afterlife which people commonly use all the time, for me was incorrect. To me it implies that this physical life is the primary life, which I have come to learn in our Spiritual Journey this is NOT the case. I prefer the term Life After Life. So where should I begin in my research of this field composed of so many disciplines?

A logical starting point was The Near Death Experience (NDE), which the psychiatrist Dr. Raymond Moody was one of the major clinical researchers in this area, and who became quite famous for his clinical contributions. It all began in 1975 with the pioneer book that was a worldwide bestseller *Life After Life.* He followed with several other books through the decades. The phenomena of NDE at times are called the Gateway to the Afterlife. Let's take a quick look back in history. Plato was the first one really to take the concept of an Afterlife quite seriously. In reality is that we survive death. So simply explained, The Near Death Experience is when the heart has stopped, meaning blood circulation has ceased, then comes the experience by "consciousness which has left the body" and describes a vast array of vivid loving lucid detailed visions. This is very different and totally opposite to a brain clouded by drugs. Keep in mind that these visions occur with no or very little brain function. The conscious mind separates from the body.

Consciousness is outside the brain. This says that physical death occurred for moments in time, but consciousness survives to tell us the story of The Other Side. Consciousness, which really is our total awareness, has left the body. What was the story that these many thousands of patients described through the decades with numerous clinicians about The Other Side? Similar stories now have been described by a vast array of physicians, medical staff and scientists within every specialty imaginable with many thousands of patients throughout several decades. These experiences are consistent throughout the world.

So what is the summary of the characteristics of a visit to The Other Side by an NDE?

Listed below is a general outline of several elements:

1) An out-of-body experience (OBE). You rise up and look down on your physical body. Heightened senses; consciousness leaves the body. You understand what is going on and you are aware of what the doctors and nurses are thinking. One enters a state of consciousness that no words could ever describe. This is NOT a dream like state. It has been described as a "hyper real state." It is more real than here. The dream is here. The true reality is there. It is like you withdraw from your body.
2) Intense and generally positive emotions or feelings, like peace and love, are the most common words used. A common statement is that "you never felt so alive as now."
3) Travel to different parts of the hospital and accurately describe conversations and experiences elsewhere in the hospital.
4) Passing into and through a tunnel. This tunnel takes you to The Other Side where there is love far beyond any love here.
5) Encountering a mystical or brilliant light.

6) Encountering deceased relatives and friends or mystical beings.

7) A sense of alteration in time and space. You are no longer limited by time. It is a state of timelessness. Time stands still.

8) A life review occurs in a panoramic, holographic setting. You see every detail, every action of your life. You feel the good and bad feelings related to others in your life. You feel their pain. This life review occurs with a light being similar to a tutor. This review is not in segments but everything is there at once.

9) Encountering otherworldly (heavenly) realms

10) Encountering or learning special knowledge. After the NDE experience many come away with what this life is about is to learn to love.

11) Encountering a boundary or barrier on The Other Side in which you must return to your body and this physical realm.

12) A voluntary or involuntary return to the body. Most of the time you return to your body and this physical realm for others in your life here.

The NDE doesn't have all these aspects, but most have several. These are the common themes of NDE. People who experience NDE no longer have a fear of death. What we call death is just a transition to another form of existence.

Skeptics have claimed several concepts, however they have been easily refuted.

I would ask the basic question that through the many decades have all these doctors and medical staff, from a wide spectrum of medical disciplines, and these many thousands of patients all be "nuts"? That is highly unlikely! Reading the massive amount of evidence and experiences leaves a rational mind with the sense that NDE are a real glimpse into The Other Side. We are talking about a database of patients into the many thousands witnessed by countless medical staff.

There is something else too, THE SHARED NDE. Loved ones' sitting by the bedside also can get the tour of The Other Side. They are healthy, not sick, thus indicating that these are not subjective hallucinations by the patient. These numerous bystanders have the same experience, the same visions. They are NOT experiencing oxygen deprivation. They are not injured in any way. Many times, the bystanders see the room fill with light and see spirits come. Plus, think about how the person having the NDE describes accurately, in detail, events and conversations in several other parts of the hospital. Then being confirmed by the medical staff who are in total shock.

With the countless NDE experiences around the world, the visions are the same across cultures and religions. All people state that the visions are DIFFERENT from their religious expectations and don't fit with what someone would imagine. The experience of the NDE has become so common that the medical community can no longer ignore them. The NDE is rational proof of an Afterlife.

There are also the phenomena of the materializations of deceased people who have appeared to countless Mediums while in front of numerous observers, and verified. These observers include scientists, royalty, and professionals of several disciplines, whose testimony is beyond any rational reproach to provide verification. These witnesses have impeccable reputations. These observations are not ghosts or apparitions. These deceased people have a complete appearance, have been hugged by loved ones, and numerous conversations occur. This alone is remarkable evidence of the survival of life after the physical body dies here in this dimension. If one does an extensive historical search, the database for the materializations of "so called" deceased people is very large.

After reading the voluminous amount of NDE medical literature, I then started researching the field of The After Death Communication (ADC). As I started to read this massive Life After Life literature two concepts truly stood out that people need to understand. FIRST, WE ALWAYS THINK THAT WE ARE A BODY WITH A SOUL. THAT IS SIMPLY NOT THE CASE. WE ARE A SOUL WITH A BODY! Think about it. That is a very big difference. The second thing people need to understand is that everything in this spiritual universe is energy. As Albert Einstein essentially said "Energy can neither be created nor destroyed; rather it can only be transformed from one form to another."

Everything is energy in this universe, and vibrates at its own unique frequency.

The ADC or in other words, how the spirit people communicate with us, occurs in several ways. After reading all the methods that spirit people communicate with us, here is a brief summary of the again massive amounts of literature and many thousands of people's experiences. The Spirit people communicate to us in a wide variety of ways. Here are some of the major types of After Death Communication:

1) Sensing or feeling the presence of a deceased person is quite common. These forms of contact can occur at any time, anywhere. They are feelings of love and comfort.
2) Auditory Communication, which is hearing a voice inside one's head or externally. The messages are received mentally and not through the ears, telepathy. One can feel their presence and also hear a message. An underlying message most of the time is that

we will be reunited again when you cross over. We will see each other again.

3) Many people have reported a physical touch countless times. Whether it is a light tap, a gentle caress, a comforting arm around the shoulder, a light kiss and more. It is a way to express emotional support and reassurance.

4) A very common one is the smell of a fragrance such as perfume, cologne, flowers with no physical source. Many times there will be a combination of sensing the Spirit presence and the smell of a fragrance.

5) Another common form of contact is the actual seeing of a departed loved one either partially or fully. One may see just the face or the entire body that appears transparent. Many times these visual appearances are coupled with verbal communication.

6) A very common form of connection is sleep state contact in a vivid dream where the mind is more receptive and relaxed. This is called a "dream visit."

7) Telephone contact by departed loved ones has extensively occurred. However, today with all the electronic communication devices, there have been a multitude of reports of Electronic Voice Phenomenon (EVP). There is a complete vast field today devoted by many to these various forms of contact where the voices of loved ones are recorded or on tape.

8) A very common form is the electronic messages sent by turning lights on and off, radios, TV's and other electrical devices being turned on and off. There is no rational reason that these instruments should be ON by themselves when the switch is in the OFF position.

9) There is a group of symbolic ADC that includes the persistent presence of butterflies, rainbows, flowers, many different species of birds, and other animals, plus a wide variety of inanimate objects.

These signs often appear spontaneously, or people have been known to pray for one from a departed loved one.

Most ADCs are joyful events with much love. They are inspired by the continuing love and concern that your deceased loved ones and friends have for you. Many times ADCs are for the protection of loved ones here in this physical plane. The massive degree of information on ADCs proves that deceased loved ones continue to exist. The comforting thought is that the separation is temporary and we will be reunited when we make the transition.

ADCs confirm there is a life after this physical death here on Earth. This phenomenon proves that death does not stop love and does not end relationships. ADC proves that life is beyond this doorway we call death.

After I examined much of the vast evidence of ADC, which involved many thousands of people, the obvious question was "can all these people be crazy or hallucinating?" A rational mind would say no. In fact with all the massive amount of evidence for NDE and ADC, which would fill up vast rooms, it actually is irrational 'not' to accept that there is definitely a life after this life and it is very active here. This was an epiphany moment for me. We are entering a whole new realm of knowledge. The quest for knowledge is always eternal.

CHAPTER 7

THE SOULPHONE FOUNDATION and MEDITATION

After my extensive research with all of the medical and scientific literature of NDE and ADC, I did extensive Internet research into the websites dealing with the numerous topics of The Afterlife. A few examples of some of these professional conferences and societies: The Original Afterlife Awareness Conference, The Afterlife Research and Education Institute, and several other organizations. Not to mention the Omega Institute, The Lilydale Assembly, and a wide spectrum of Spiritual Churches throughout this country and the world. I was impressed by all the available sources of information.

As I was doing Internet research, I came across a website titled The Soulphone Foundation. I was quite curious since the title of this organization was intriguing. This is a group of highly respected individuals in the disciplines of Medicine, Science and Spiritualism, dedicated to communicating with the spirit people or as they call them the Post Material Persons (PMPs) on The Other Side by various forms of highly advanced technology.

There is a very long credible history, supported by numerous publications in peer review journals, of great success in the communication with the spirit people on The Other Side, backed up by several avenues of evidence. The experimental design has been impeccable, in which the path of the evidence is followed, wherever it may lead. The intensive research is so rigorous that the example is set as a standard for all other investigators in these fields. The evidence determines the conclusions, not human prejudice or bias. Their database has grown quite large over numerous years. This is the perfect example of the ultimate merging of science, medicine and spiritualism. Some day in the near future, people will be able to call their loved ones and friends on The Other Side.

This dedicated group of people are doing a great service to humanity and should be greatly admired. Not only learning a great deal from my conversations with people in this Foundation but it introduced and started me on the path of meditations, to connect with my eternal heart Felecia on The Other Side. I discovered a whole world of CDs, websites, and computer links that were available to me at nominal expense to practice meditation. I will always have great gratitude for the people of the Soulphone Foundation for introducing me to the power of meditation.

That is such a key word 'practice' when it comes to meditation and the hopes of connection with spirit people. It requires mind focus, perseverance, discipline, relaxation and lots of practice with a never give up attitude. Your intention and belief in the Afterlife has to be absolute and unwavering. Meditation is a doorway to people truly finding out who they really are as spirit beings, a glimpse into the soul and heart. Most importantly, your loved ones on The Other Side have to have a great desire to connect with you! Communication is always a two way street.

CHAPTER 8

THE FIRST CONNECTION WITH MEDITATION

Now it was early April in 2019 and a number of things were going on. The first time I did a formal meditation it turned out to be a turning point in my life and the Spiritual Journey with my Felecia and I. Here I am early April was my first Meditation. The only thing I can say is WOW. I told her out loud and wrote on a card by her picture that we had an appointment for a meditation and visitation. They hear and see everything here. I used a specific chair in the dining room and several photographs of her with one single white candle in front of the pictures. It is recommended to have a specific personal item of the spirit person you are attempting to connect with. So I had her wedding garter from our 1977 wedding. Both of us always had a great sense of humor. Having the garter was appropriate for us. We were such a comedy team.

All distractions from the outside world were removed and just faded away and disappeared. I said a prayer; I am partial to an Our Father, just my Catholic upbringing. I asked her, and my Spirit Guides, and Angels, especially Michael Archangel and St. Theresa for her support and their help that we would have a wonderful meditation and connection. Please note that throughout this book I use God and Source, interchangeably. I totally relaxed with deep breathing exercises that slowed down the mind and silenced all that brain chatter. My mind entered an altered state of expanded awareness that I will explain later.

About ten minutes into the meditation my girl made her presence known by strong waves of warmth and tingling tremors throughout my whole body. The waves of spirit energy of love were coming in groups of 2 and 3. At times my whole body "rocked." Many times the waves of spirit energy were so strong they became tangible. My eyes started to tear. Several times I had to brace myself. At other times my whole body contracted the energy was so powerful. It lasted about 30 minutes. I said to myself Holy Shit!!! I was in awe and totally surprised. It was a total blending or merging of our energy.

These powerful waves of spirit energy blending with my energy ONLY occurred when I had images of her. Anyone or anything else, there was NOTHING! This magnificent powerful energy response was ONLY with her and nothing else. What I learned later was that this is CLAIRSENTIENCE defined as the ability to feel. This is one of the major ways the spirit people communicate with us, their presence of spirit love energy. During this amazing experience I said out loud my love for her. When it was over; I was exhausted and dizzy. It absolutely was HER, that was definite.

Here I am, all my life a very rational, analytical, objective person in medicine and science, the ultimate skeptic. I could not make this stuff up if I tried. I did not know what this was until I did research and talked with several people 'in the know' in these fields. These powerful constant waves of spirit energy were as real as flesh and blood. Here I am, the ultimate "prove it to me guy" and Felecia sure did that in a spectacular fashion. My girl, was and is, truly amazing. I never experienced anything like this in my entire life. I am not alone. I did not have to rely on hope to communicate with her. It was the real deal. What I realized is that we actually have a real relationship.

What I experienced with that first connection by meditation with Felecia, I would challenge any skeptic. Three years ago if I would have been describing an experience of this nature I would have said put a net over my head and take me away. What are you nuts? This was a major breakthrough! Her desire to connect with me was as strong as my wish to communicate with her. I actually, for the first time, had real hope of communicating with her and being with her. As I was doing and practicing meditations other events were occurring at the same time in my life.

CHAPTER 9

EMDR (EYE MOVEMENT DESENSITIZATION AND REPROCESSING) THERAPY

Now what is EMDR therapy? It is a psychotherapy technique used to relieve psychological stress. It has been shown to be an effective treatment for trauma and post-traumatic stress disorder (PTSD).

Now remember, through all of this, I am dealing with the trauma of my girl's last moments, the terrible thoughts, images, flash backs, my guilt being in the medical and science profession and not being able to save her. Finally, I was dealing with the grief of losing a dear loved one who was the most important person in my life. After some research, I decided to undergo EMDR therapy.

For approximately the last 20 years, it was discovered that trauma and grief of this magnitude is actually organic, in the right hemisphere of the brain where all our emotions, creativity, intuition, imagination and psychic properties are stored. In other words, the right hemisphere of the brain is not physiologically functioning the way it should. There is a paralysis of function. Since it is organic, at this point counseling is a total waste of time and money. All the words in the world will not relieve the lack of physiological functioning in the right hemisphere of the brain. One is just wasting their money and time with counseling in this type of situation.

Techniques practiced by many psychotherapists in EMDR therapy is simultaneously stimulating both left and right hemispheres of the brain in several ways, to relieve the physiological stagnant functioning of the right side. It is a bilateral stimulation of both hemispheres. A reorientation of perception develops when the hemispheres are alternately sped up. Simultaneous stimulation occurs by rapid eye following movement, with auditory and quantitative analysis of the worst thoughts and images. Incorporated in all this is a detailed history of events subjected to in depth analysis. It is very intense and emotional which is performed for approximately eight hours. The hemispheres of the brain go into high gear to alleviate the "stasis." It is all about the processing of the brain. Much of this science was discovered with 9-11 patients pertaining to the lack of physiological functioning of the right hemisphere of the brain. After doing research, and calling psychotherapists in this country, I settled on one in Seattle, Washington, who was a teacher to many therapists in this country. Why go to a student when you can go to the teacher?

Prior to visiting this psychotherapist I returned to the Medium in Lilydale, who had helped me start this Spiritual Journey back in December. It was now April one week prior to departing for Seattle.

When I arrived at the Medium in Lilydale, she said Felecia was around her for several days, and waiting for me. Felecia indicated that I would be going out West and she would be with me. The biggest revelation was that Felecia said I would be having a Spiritual Rebirth, like a Near Death Experience (NDE) with my EMDR therapy in Seattle. Felecia knew I had pneumonia back in March. My girl pointed to her wedding ring and said we are still married! She certainly got that right. My girl is not alone. She is with my family and hers and at peace. I am the one who got left behind. We are together but separated by a wall. She is at peace and we will advance together and always communicate. Nothing will stop us from being connected.

When I left this Medium for a second time, my trip to Seattle for the EMDR Therapy was to be a Spiritual Rebirth, like a Near Death Experience, and my girl will be with me. My curiosity was burning inside of me as to what the nature was going to be of my Spiritual Rebirth.

CHAPTER 10

THE FATEFUL TRIP TO SEATTLE

I was still sleeping on the couch in the family room at night. I had not yet slept in our bedroom. I had a very early morning flight to take me on my journey across the country to Seattle, WA. I set an alarm but Felecia wanted to make sure I woke up in time so she hit me several times with her perfume, that beautiful, mild, soft smelling fragrance. She stayed with me every moment of this experience on the West Coast. When the airplane landed in Seattle, I turned on my cell phone and 11:11 immediately appeared.

Now for several months I have been constantly seeing everywhere, on every imaginable clock, watch, 11:11. I learned that this was a very powerful text message from the spiritual realm. It was so frequent I actually started to pay attention. I began researching what was the spiritual meaning of 11:11, and found that it is a deceased loved one sending you a message and you have been called to awaken. You are on the right path and to take action. Also, over time I was receiving 4:44 quite often too. This is considered the angel numbers. Again in my research these are divine text messages from the higher realms. I am protected and guided. I am on the path of awakening. Just stay on this path of discovery and everything will be OK. My intuition was telling me that this trip to Seattle would be a transforming event. Boy, was I ever right on that one. The stage was set for whatever was coming.

It was Holy Thursday, April 18, 2019, the start of the Easter Celebration in the Christian Calendar. The psychotherapist picked me up at my hotel to travel to her home office a few minutes away.

Immediately she said to me that she felt Felecia around her all that morning. The EMDR therapy started that morning. We set up white candles, wedding pictures of my beautiful girl, her wedding garter as represented by something of hers and the top of the wedding cake. The wedding top had a bride and groom kissing on a chair under a white archway. Her wedding garter as something of hers was our mutual sense of humor. We were a comedy team my Tweek and I. My beautiful girl was ready for the therapy session. Felecia helped me with the therapy. She was with me and came through very strong by her Clairsentience. At times her waves of spirit energy of love were so powerful it literally was overwhelming. Felecia is a powerhouse of love.

The EMDR therapy was very intense all day with aggressive multiple simultaneous stimulations of both brain hemispheres. At the end of a long day of psychotherapy, I asked Felecia two questions after she was there coming through strong by Clairsentience. "What do you want to say to me or impart to me before we close?" Felecia said: the children, take care of them, all of them, the children, help the children. She followed it up with strong Clairsentience waves of energy. It is the children. She confirmed it three times. I now can distinguish her thoughts in my mind that come through loud and clear from my own thoughts. In the last two months I thought I heard her but now I do know it is her. It is all about listening.

The second question I asked her is, "How do I celebrate each holiday or special day without you?" My Tweek said celebrate, I'll be there! She hammered me with this 4 to 5 times. I said OK OK WOW WOW OK, I GOT IT. This confirmed that I could hear her voice clearly in my mind. I now can detect auditory with Felecia. This is termed Clairaudience, to hear or better to listen.

I immediately started to notice later that night, after the first day of therapy, a softening of the horrible images and thoughts of my girl's last moments. My psychotherapist mentioned to me as time passes in the next month or so the trauma, images and thoughts will fade further as the brain continues with its reprocessing. I had to return for a second day of EMDR therapy because of my extensive guilt of being in the medical profession and not being able to save her.

The psychotherapist used Bluetooth in her car to talk to friends by phone. It had been working fine, however on Thursday, the first day, all of a sudden it stopped working for no reason. So I was in my hotel room the second day, the morning of Friday, April 19th, and I asked Felecia out loud did you "knock out" her Bluetooth? Felecia immediately responded yes because it is about safety, you were in the car. Last night, Thursday, the computers in the psychotherapist's home were working on the Internet even though the Wi-Fi was out. The therapist said this never happened before. My girl always liked to play with electronics, so this did not surprise me in the least. By the end of this two day ordeal I would bet the therapist was very glad to see Felecia and I depart.

Now it is the second day of therapy, Good Friday, April 19, 2019, one of the holiest days for Christians. At the end of this day my life would change forever. The psychotherapist picked me up at 11:00 AM and we arrived at her home office to continue the therapy. I glanced at my cell phone and it again displayed 11:11. Felecia was waiting for us. I could feel her. I set up her wedding pictures, the top of our wedding cake, her wedding garter, and lit candles. Felecia immediately made her presence known throughout the four hour session by Clairsentience, very strong waves of spirit energy. The focus of the therapy today was on my guilt in being in the medical profession but not being able to save her. We listed all the things I had guilt of in that terrible 15 month tribulation. As the therapy continued I made the statement "It was not meant to be." Immediately all hell broke lose. Felecia gave me powerful waves of Clairsentience energy in affirmation. It literally rocked me.

She said several times in my mind that it was OK. What was amazing is the therapist received chills down her whole body from head to toes when that statement was made. We were shocked because this indicated the utmost validation that this is what Felecia was trying to communicate to us, that it was not meant to be.

Now remember when I had a reading by the Medium in Lilydale the week before, that Felecia said I would have something like a Near Death Experience (NDE) in Seattle; a Rebirth, a Spiritual Vision. Keep this in Mind because I never gave Reincarnation any thought; so here it goes. I entered a state in which I was saying things that I totally had no control over. Describing images, pictures from long ago. It was like Felecia was describing things to me and I was a conduit for her. Since she crossed over she learned about this past life together. I was periodically crying. Long ago images were coming through in which I was talking with no control. We were together on an ornately carved white stone bench. There was ocean, white mountains, and sun. The mountains were shear and sharp. My Felecia was so beautiful in which she wore shear white veils as dress in ancient Rome/Greece times. She was all in white. My Felecia had a crown wreath of small beautiful white flowers in her hair. She had several bracelets on each wrist. I could see the ornate design of the bracelets and the very vivid colors. She was so beautiful and voluptuous. She glowed. I had a red uniform with a yellow bronze breastplate on. The sun reflected off my shield and breastplate. The shield had a side profile of an eagle. We were both young. I had images of my muscular body. I was a soldier. I felt what was coming through that Felecia was high in society. You could feel our deep love. I was leaving saying goodbye for some expedition, like it was my duty. It was so amazing, the image of her beautiful smile.

What came through is I lost her long ago and I did not want to lose her a second time in this time. No matter what, somewhere in time we will find each other again.

What was very important was just before the description of long ago started, the therapist received for the second time a series of strong chills starting at the top of her head and traveling down her whole body. Again, validating from Felecia what occurred long ago was real and true from her. This would explain why she told the Medium just before this trip to Seattle, I would have a Near Death Experience, a REBIRTH, a SPIRITUAL VISION. This would explain why our relationship is so deep, like twins, in many respects because we were together long ago. So there you have it, totally unexpected except she knew what was going to happen. The therapist and I are not crazy. The therapist said this is REINCARNATION.

I never gave reincarnation a thought. Reincarnation was just a word to me. My head was spinning. As I was flying back from the West Coast I was totally surprised, shocked. I was not sure what to do next. This transformation that started in the West coast would change our Spiritual Journey forever. It would change my life forever.

CHAPTER 11

A STORY ABOUT ENERGY

While I was thinking about Felecia and I sharing a past life together in ancient times, I was practicing and experiencing numerous forms of meditation. I learned meditations of this nature takes much practice, mind focus, perseverance, great relaxation through deep breathing techniques and discipline to eliminate distractions. One must slow down the brain and silence the chatter in one's mind. My motto was simple "Never quit just keep going." I am the type of person who adds new meaning to the word relentless. If there is a brick wall between an objective and me on the other side, if I have to, I will go through that brick wall. It is a totally relentless attitude. No matter how many times you fall, you just keep getting up. It is getting up that is important.

Now there are several concepts one needs to understand in making the connection with a loved one on The Other Side. It is an understanding of some basic principles in neurology and quantum physics. Everything around us that we can detect and not detect with our senses is quantum physics. In other words, it is our total world surrounding us in every way, at every level.

As derived from numerous sources music tones have been developed which cause a rapid synchronization of both the left and right hemispheres of the brain. This allows one to achieve altered or expanded states of awareness during meditation. There are five general states of brain wave activity namely: Gamma, Beta, Alpha, Theta and Delta. The brain wave activity are measured in Hz like a radio. Gamma is the fastest of brain wave activity and frequency, about 38 to 42 Hz.

Then comes Beta activity, which dominates our normal waking consciousness, 12 to 38 Hz. The Alpha state brain waves are quietly flowing thoughts in a meditative state. Alpha is the resting state of the brain, in 8 to 12 Hz. The next state is Theta. This state occurs in sleep and is dominant in deep meditation. This is a twilight state, dream state, intuition, 3 to 8 Hz. Finally, is the Delta state, which are slow and generated in deep meditation and dreamless sleep, 0.5 to 3 Hz.

This whole process in meditation is to slow down the brain, silence the continual chatter of the brain to enter states of expanded awareness and deep meditation. The objective is to enter the Alpha and Theta altered states of awareness. The spirit people are then able to impress upon our consciousness with their thoughts, images, feelings, scents, words, emotions and sounds. In other words, in the Beta brain state the noise level is too high for the Spirit people to impress upon our consciousness. There is simply too much noise in our brains in normal waking consciousness. The noise will drown out any attempt by spirit to connect with us. Thus, when the brain is slowed down in these other states, a connection can be detected and made with spirit.

Now let us talk about some simple quantum physics. This is a conversation about energy. Everything in this spiritual universe is one form of energy or another. The foundation of this universe is the transformation, concentration, manipulation and manifestation of energy. Using psychic information is all about energy. Everything is energy vibrating at its own unique frequency. Inside our shells of skin and bones we are spiritual beings made up of energy. The power of thought; or thought energy is central in this spiritual universe. There is an instantaneous language of energy. Each thought has its own energy signature. It is the power of thought and intention. Everything that is done, deeds, emotions, words, thoughts have their own unique frequency of vibration.

How we connect with the spirit people on The Other Side is a process known as The Quickening. The Other Side is the numerous higher energy vibration dimensions termed the Astral Planes around Earth. Through various forms of meditation, we in the basic physical Earth realm raise our vibration frequencies. The spirit people in the Astral realm lower their vibration frequencies and there is a blending or merging of energy. No matter what form of meditation is used, Felecia and I blend our energy on a daily basis. We merge our energy across dimensions. Her favorite form of communication is through Clairsentience (to feel). At times it is simply overwhelming and very powerful. It can be so strong, it can take my breath away and I simply cannot talk.

I finally deciphered that Clairsentience is spirit energy, waves of love, and the most powerful energy in this entire spiritual universe. There is one religion and that religion is love. I know, for several reasons, her Clairsentience is very real. It all makes sense, spirit is alive and well with bodies of energy. Plus, spirit has their total consciousness, at a higher level, total you, total personality. Everything that is them is totally intact. Something to keep in mind that I was the ultimate skeptic, all my life in medicine and science. I am always questioning, testing, and challenging. I certainly don't have that nonsense of feel good wishful thinking, hallucinations and delusions. I always try to use the ultimate of humanly possible in rational, objective, analytical thought. I never would have dreamed years ago I would be writing things of this nature. People reject these concepts out of fear, prejudice, arrogance and ignorance. However, if your mind is closed, how are you going to learn new things? It is so easy to get fooled by the touch of our flesh. You want to be an open-minded skeptic; not a closed minded one.

When Felecia is not around me the difference is very dramatic because there is ABSOLUTELY NOTHING. When I test by having thoughts and images of her that should generate a major Clairsentience reaction, there is nothing since she is NOT there. Felecia's spirit energy waves of Clairsentience at times is overwhelming with thoughts and images of ONLY HER; however with any thoughts or images of anyone or anything else there is no response, nothing. There are numerous times when I do something she really likes that she sends me an overpowering Clairsentience blast of spirit energy. I never knew what Clairsentience was until I started to have these spirit energy waves and then did research. If I wanted to I could not begin to "fake this," even if I tried real hard.

Through the months I have developed a daily routine in my meditations and visitations with my Felecia. Always in the morning I first open my seven main Chakras. Chakra means wheel in India. Chakras are spinning energy wheels. They run upward along the spinal cord with energy running in front and back. The Chakras allow the determination of subtle psychic energy. The universe is filled with psychic energy. The Chakras are the connection between your physical body and your Aura; which is the electromagnetic energy field around all things. Each Chakra has a distinct auric color and function. These are the contact points between the physical and spiritual worlds. Always remember, we are spirit, in human form. Our spiritual energy breathes life into our physical body. Extensive literature has been written about Chakras over time. Exercises in opening Chakras most definitely enhance psychic and spiritual abilities. After my Chakras are open then I proceed to mind focus exercises to enhance my Clairaudience (to hear or listen), Clairsentience (to feel) and Clairvoyance (to see). At this point I proceed to a specific meditation and my girl never lets me down, she always comes through immediately and we have a wonderful connection and visit.

I started thinking more and more about this revelation of reincarnation and what I was going to do about it. Events occurred the next several months that shattered all my beliefs in life, that this physical life here was not the true reality. People believe that this present life is all there is, and nothing else. We could NOT be more wrong.

CHAPTER 12

PURSUING REINCARNATION AND EVENTS IN THE LATE SPRING AND SUMMER OF 2019

After learning about the connection Felecia and I had to past lives with Reincarnation, I then had to figure out what would be the next steps to pursue this road in our Spiritual Journey. After doing research and talking to various medical and scientific people in these fields, the name Dr. Brian Weiss kept resurfacing. After doing research on this world famous psychiatrist and neurologist, it was apparent that he was one of the key people in this discipline of Reincarnation and Past Lives Regression Therapy. Dr. Weiss has written numerous best selling books on these topics, of which I have read and he has had extensive media exposure through the decades. In order to gain more knowledge on this extensive discipline of Reincarnation, I decided to register for his week long course that he gives a few times a year at the Omega Institute in Rhinebeck, New York. The course was scheduled for early September. I looked forward to this course with great excitement and anticipation in the pursuit of more knowledge on the past lives Felecia and I have shared together. This was such a totally unexpected development in our Spiritual Journey.

With the daily meditations and visits by my girl, my spiritual senses were dramatically improving and getting stronger. It was like my central nervous system was becoming very sensitized to her presence and her energy frequencies. At times I could sense that I could hear her. I started to hear her periodically.

As the meditations were progressing, several incredible amazing events occurred. The first event that is unforgettable involves the hanging of a large picture on our living room wall. I was putting up one of our son's wedding pictures. It was a big picture and was on a high hook. I was lazy; I should have gotten a small stool and pulled out the couch to have better access and height to place this picture. However, it was a difficult hook to catch on the wall and it was high. I PHYSICALLY SIMPLY COULD NOT PLACE THIS PICTURE ON THE WALL. My head was hanging between my outstretched arms and I said out loud "ohh Felecia, you know me, ohh Felecia." I felt her around me with very strong energy. Then all of a sudden a force lifted the picture out of my hands and placed it in the exact position on this difficult hook. I actually felt this force lift the picture and place it in the correct position. My girl heard me and was there to help me place this picture on the living room wall. She is always around me. I can always count on her. Isn't she something? My love for her has no limit.

Another amazing incident involved my wedding ring. For months after Felecia passed on or Crossed the Veil, I was looking for my wedding ring. As it is common when one gets older, you gain weight and your fingers get fat, many of us know "the fat fingers syndrome" where rings do not fit anymore. So here I am thinking "where the hell is my wedding ring?". I had her wedding ring on a chain around my neck and I wanted to add my ring so our rings would be together close to my heart.

I had not slept in our bedroom for seven months since Felecia transitioned to The Other Side. It was a Saturday morning and I went upstairs to clean and organize our bedroom. Now Felecia's white jewelry chest is a large free standing one. Through the previous months I had emptied out all the jewelry or I thought so. The top of the chest appeared to be solid; but as I was moving the chest to clean, it was a false top, and it opened. There it was my wedding ring. Plus, several priceless sentimental lockets and other jewelry when we were dating back in the 1970's. I was so happy. I placed our rings together on the chain by my heart. Her ring fit perfectly inside my ring. Now they were together only to be separated when I Crossed the Veil to return HOME. For all of us, this is our true HOME.

A little bit later, I went downstairs to the family room where there was a large photograph of her above the TV; I said out loud "Honey I found my wedding ring, now both are together by my heart." I was so excited to share this joy with her. I always talked out loud to her. I proceeded to turn on the TV below where I had the channel of Easy Listening Music on. Instantly, the song that started to play was our wedding song "I Won't Last a Day Without You" by The Carpenters. Now of all the countless songs in this world our wedding song started to play at that moment in time. The probability of this occurring is astronomically low. As it is said, there are no coincidences in the Spirit World. So on June 22, 2019 Felecia and I were remarried. We had our wedding rings reunited, our wedding song started to play and I did dance to it in the family room. We only needed the wedding cake and the band. A synchronicity of this magnitude defies any law of probability. My girl, all the time, does amazing things. She has surpassed all my expectations of wonderment.

I had a large photograph of Felecia at 50 years old that we used for the wake and funeral announcements. She was so beautiful; but then again she always was so very beautiful, regardless of her age. Even when she was so sick, she still was totally Felecia. I took this photograph to the photography department at a local Walgreens to be enlarged and copies made and framed for all at the family homes. This was another tribute to honor her, by the family. As the lady in the photography department was working on the enlargements on the computer ALL OF A SUDDEN VERY STRONG WAVES OF CLAIRSENTIENCE SPIRIT ENERGY HIT ME. I MEAN LITERALLY HIT ME!!! The energy waves were so powerful I had to sit down. What it told me was that Felecia very much liked what I was doing in making a picture of her and giving it to all the family. These very strong waves of Clairsentience Spirit Energy never happen except in meditation and visitation sessions. However, I am always sitting down and had to brace myself at times in anticipation. I do get subtle gentle waves at times during the day if I say something to her or have certain thoughts of her, but not like this. The power of her Clairsentience energy is a direct function of her emotions, when she really likes something; or not and "gets pissed off." I always joke by saying you don't want to "piss off" my girl; you may not know what hit you. At times I actually can sense her moods as a feeling of the Clairsentience intensity. The power of this connection is a result of love that will not be denied across dimensions and the intention of relentless intensity. There are times when I can locate her in a room. She hears and sees everything, as reflected by the Spirit World. Our spiritual connection advanced to the point where I could always sense when she was around me. I am amazed at times on how acute my psychic and spiritual sensitivities have become. It is a great awakening of my spiritual senses. When I want to confirm her presence I do what I now call "ALPHA CHECKS." Using various breathing techniques I enter into the alpha brain state of expanded awareness in moments, and then will determine instantly her presence or not. At times we don't require anything anymore. I don't have to be in a meditative state. I have become very sensitive to her presence. The Spirit World knows what we are doing and they know what they are doing.

A word about thought and telepathy. I noticed that as Felecia and I advanced in our meditations and visitations I was able to communicate with her by telepathy. THOUGHT RULES, once we Cross the Veil to the infinity of the higher energy dimensions, worlds and realities. IT IS THE POWER OF THOUGHT. Nothing is hidden. There are no secrets. Remember, a 'thought' is vibrating energy with its own specific energy frequency or signature. Felecia is just a thought away. We are our thoughts in the higher realms. In our physical world, our thoughts will get stored in our electromagnetic field of the Aura and or the Soul. The energy power of projected thought is one of the foundations of the universe. Travel can be by thought projection; just by thinking of a place, you are there. If you want to build something, like a home or gardens around your home, or anything else, you just have to think it through and it is there. On The Other Side, a soul goes from thought to reality and nothing in between. It is so true on The Other Side that you are your thoughts.

No matter what my daily daytime activities are, she at numerous times always is with me. Whether I travel, go on a trip, go to the grocery store, or to visit family, sitting in a booth at a restaurant, family events or just being outdoors. I do my "ALPHA CHECKS" and I pick her up immediately and many times locate her. With special situations such as when I was moving out some of our furniture and personal effects we had over several decades to some of our children, my girl always made her presence known in these very difficult days of the dismantling of our personal possessions to family. As our Spiritual Journey progressed, I started to share with family and close friends what I was learning in an attempt to help them in the relief of grief. I hope that within our hearts, it truly did help them.

All forms of cemeteries have existed for numerous millennia to honor and pay tribute to the "so called" dead with the thought that they are there. At first when Felecia Crossed the Veil I would visit the cemetery every few days and sit on a small stool and talk while crying to her. I was thinking early on that she actually was there. As my girl and I progressed in our Spiritual Journey during the many passing months I started to realize, now wait she is NOT at the cemetery, she is with me! What is at the cemetery is just THE REMAINS of the body, just the skin and bones, from that particular life. As it is said the butterfly leaves behind the remains of the cocoon of the caterpillar. What ultimately occurred was that we both would go to the cemetery to pay our respects and look at the beautiful and very expensive monument that was placed at the cemetery for both of us. As I would stand in front of our monument at the cemetery I would do an "ALPHA CHECK" and she was always there with me, standing with me looking at the gravesite. At times I would laugh at the irony and humor of the situation. I sensed with my spiritual intuition that she would find humor in the situation and laugh too. At some point I would say let's go and we would leave the gravesite and I would immediately convert back to the Beta brain state; normal waking consciousness. One could never drive in the Alpha state, because you would most likely end up a tree.

What was truly incredible was that as time passed, my Felecia started to bring other deceased family members with her to visit. The possibility existed that they came on their own, but it really does not matter. My Dad and Felecia were close; and I was close with my Dad. As time passed about an average of once per week, this is what occurred. I would have the TV on in the mornings on the channel of Easy Listening as I was drinking my morning coffee. Many times I was in emotional bad shape with the countless memories of 43 years going through my mind. Will I ever reach the state of ONLY totally cherishing those years with her and not to have all the anger, bitterness, pain, trauma, suffering, loss and grief? I simply don't know. What I do know is that Felecia was the best thing that ever happened to me in this life and all the other lives, for all eternity. She was a blessing and a gift for all eternity. I learned after talking to many in the know, in these numerous fields related to Spiritualism, that the Clairsentience that Felecia and I shared was truly a GIFT, a BLESSING, since it occurs but it is on the rare side. I started to believe that this was truly a Gift, a Blessing from God to both of us. An analogy of Clairsentience is like humidity, you cannot see it, nor hear it but you sure can feel it!

Now getting back to my Dad, he always smoked cigars; he was never without a cigar. That was his trademark. So sitting at the breakfast table drinking my morning coffee, on the TV Easy Listening channel would start a song of the 1930's and 40's that was one of my Dad's favorite songs. I would say out loud "Hey Dad that was one of your favorite songs." I would walk into the family room where the TV is and immediately a very strong cigar smoke smell came across my nose and mouth and persisted for awhile. It definitely was the smell of his cigars. I started crying and thanked Felecia and Dad. I think Felecia brings Dad to comfort me. It worked because it does help me. I thanked both of them out loud and cried. I am not nuts. This is not wishful thinking. You have his favorite songs and cigar smoke smell at the same time.

As the Spiritual Journey for Tweek and I was continually advancing, and discovering our spiritual selves as time went on more and more, the date was approaching early in September for a trip to The Omega Institute with Dr. Brian Weiss and Reincarnation. The time was set for this new road in our Spiritual Journey.

CHAPTER 13

THE NEW ROAD TO REINCARNATION

It was early September 2019 that the course I attended on Past Lives Regression Therapy was taking place at the Omega Institute in New York by Dr. Brian Weiss, psychiatrist and neurologist. The Omega Institute is in a beautiful setting in the Hudson Valley. The accommodations and food were exceptional. This was a week-long course. Dr. Brian Weiss has 40 years of clinical experience with an impeccable medical history in Past Lives Regression Therapy (Reincarnation). He has written numerous books on the subject and has been on many TV programs. The class size was 150 people, his smallest class. There was a significant waiting list for this course, so I felt very fortunate to attend. The class was about 60% International and 40% from the USA. People came from all parts of the globe: Japan, China, throughout Asia, Western Europe, Russia and South America. Every part of this world we live in they came to hear this man speak. This was a highly educated, intellectual group of professionals from numerous disciplines. I was thinking about doctors from across the world, flying all this way to attend his course.

A great amount of knowledge was communicated in this course. Basic information was given on the conscious and subconscious mind. The conscious mind contains all of our thoughts, memories, feelings and wishes of which we are aware of at any given moment. The conscious mind is less than 10% of brain function. The subconscious mind operates without your awareness and you have no control over it. Over 90% of our brain function is the subconscious mind. It absorbs and is a reservoir of information that does not pass through the conscious mind.

Extensive attention was given to the concept of hypnosis. The AMA has recognized hypnosis as a valid method, since 1958. A simple definition of hypnosis is a focused, concentration of the mind in a very RELAXED state. There are numerous techniques and forms of hypnosis. The key word in hypnosis is RELAXATION. The progressive relaxation hypnosis procedure was used during the week, plus other techniques. The central issue is all about pulling information, specifically MEMORIES, OUT OF YOUR SUBCONSCIOUS MIND. I think we all have this Hollywood impression from movies and TV, of a guy waving a watch in front of your face and you are getting sleepy nonsense. It is nothing like that. Many psychiatrists now have proven over several years using thousands of patients is that a patient with a neurosis or phobias often is a result of a traumatic experience from a past life. Once the traumatic experience in a past life is revealed there is a high probability the neurosis or phobias will disappear. The thesis is that all our past lives are stored in our subconscious mind. That is where all the records are kept. More and more psychiatrists are using Past Lives Regression Therapy to treat neurosis or phobias.

Hypnosis simply pulls memories from our past lives out of our subconscious mind. Remember that there is a separation, or some call them amnesia blocks, between the subconscious mind, with all our past lives memories and the conscious mind because we have to function in this life. There is no time travel or nonsense like that. Past lives regression therapy by hypnosis is simply pulling out memories from the subconscious mind.

The central question is why do we have past lives? Why does our spirit reincarnate into a new body? There are volumes of information on this from countless sources. It is all about the evolution of the soul. The improvement or betterment of the soul in spirituality in gaining greater, pure love, compassion, forgiveness, charity, gratitude, understanding, and experiencing all the different manifestations of love. All souls are on a learning curve, where lessons have to be learned, debts to be paid from previous lives, karma in action. One is simply not going to accomplish this in one lifetime. That is simply impossible. One is simply not going to get it right in one lifetime. You may return in one life, for example, with an emphasis on compassion or forgiving. It is all about the elevation of the spirituality of the soul. It is the understanding of our true nature, who we really are. The soul is our real self. This is not about the body, nor the brain, but our true, authentic you. The soul is what you are. It is the purposeful, powerful essence of you.

The central question is when a person is under a form of hypnosis, are the memories from the subconscious mind of past lives REAL? How does one separate these memories from imagination, fantasy, or daydreaming? It was explained that after many decades of clinical experience, with several thousands of patients, that the criteria that the memories of past lives from the subconscious mind are real:

1) The memories repeat constantly over a period of time.
2) There is significant emotion with these memories.
3) As memories of a past life progress over time, many more details occur. These memories become a lot more detailed and vivid especially with color, as more memories are slowly released from the subconscious mind.

Imagination, fantasy, daydreaming have none of these characteristics. They come then are gone, no emotion is involved.

An interesting point was briefly discussed about why there is no reference to Reincarnation in the Bible, Holy Scriptures? When Christianity became a recognized religion in the Roman Empire in 313 AD by the first Roman Emperor who converted to Christianity, Constantine, ALL REFERENCES TO REINCARNATION WERE REMOVED

BY THE ROMANS IN THE HOLY SCRIPTURES AND BIBLE. The reason the Romans did this was because they were worried that if the people realized they were eternal, and could return here, then this would cause a problem in control of the people. The people would realize that they could not be hurt. The Romans were all about control of the populace. It was politics, as simple as that!

The organized religions of the world, with the exception of a few, do not mention Reincarnation. Organized religions are in the control business based on guilt and punishment, and by the way give us your money. If there were an endorsement of reincarnation, the religious power brokers would lose control of the flock, their power base, positions and money. Dates change, places change, names change but through the ages human nature never changes.

The procedure used for the hypnosis was the common progressive relaxation procedure. As a composite of three sessions with witnesses the following occurred. However, these images described below have been repeating over several months in meditations. There was much emotion and tears, indicating the images were real and repeating over time. There were lives in 11th century Mongolia and 17th century England. However, the dominant one was about 300-200 BC in ancient Rome.

As the floodgates opened up, this is what was revealed. One is always asked first to look down and see what shoes one has on or not because this tells the time period. The images: my feet have brown sandals with ties around my ankles, up my lower legs. The dirt is soft and a reddish brown color. The sandals are made from animal hide. I am short with a muscular body, my torso, arms, hands were strong and muscular. I have a red uniform with metal petals, and a bronze breastplate of yellow, with sword and shield. The sun was reflecting off my breast plate. My shield has a profile of an eagle. My hand has rings on it. The rings have significance. I see my face. I have long black hair, pushed back. My sword is on the short side. The name Claudius keeps coming through, being repeated Claudius. It is just prior to battle, and then the battle occurs. It feels like the last battle for me. There is dust, dirt kicking up in the distance in the wake of an invading army. We are outnumbered. My son Jason appears as one of the soldiers and asks what do we do? I shout a command "Centurions close ranks," battle wedge. Another son of mine James is on horseback with a black helmet on, it has a nose guard down the middle. I have a black horse, the sweat on the horse is glistening in the sunlight, its nostrils are flaring. The eyes of my horse are intense on fire. I turn the horse towards the battle. Blood is running down my arm. We are the Guard, We Protect. We now fight for each other, shoulder to shoulder. There are bodies everywhere. I am looking down on the battlefield. I am floating.

Images of my Felecia, her name in this time; I do not know. She is so beautiful and voluptuous. She is dressed in white veils with several colorful ornate bracelets on each wrist. She has a circular wreath of small white flowers in her hair. She has a worried, fearful look on her face. She is walking fast and then running. The wind is blowing hard. This is my last day in this lifetime.

There are more fast images of our life together. We live in a white stone home, two children, a girl about 5 with black curly hair and an older boy about 10 with blond hair. We are sitting at the dinner table. Felecia is by a fire pit making flat breads. There are large brown wooden flat paddles.

We hold hands often; we are walking over a bridge. We are sitting on a very ornate white stone bench in a garden. I am in my soldier's uniform.

My Felecia is giving birth to our baby. I push back the white veils to see her in bed with our baby. My mother is around with some kind of headdress on. I lost my Felecia in that lifetime and now in our present one again.

I now see myself with white robes and sandals walking up many steps before this critical battle. I am walking down a stone street. I arrived at our home. It is a white stone modest home. Felecia is in the shadow of the doorway waiting for me. She is so beautiful. I feel we are happy.

There are more personal images but this will suffice. Once the images are released from the subconscious to the conscious mind you will remember everything.

It is important to note that during the hypnosis sessions, every time I had images of my Felecia, she was hitting me with her waves of Clairsentience, pure spirit energy of love.

There you have it. On Good Friday, April 19th while receiving EMDR therapy in Seattle, Washington, my Felecia alerted me to the fact that we shared past lives together. I never gave Reincarnation any thought or credence.

It was just a word to me. I always wondered why we were so close, at times, "twin like." Within two weeks of the EMDR therapy I enrolled in this course. I came to the Omega Institute with questions seeking answers, and no expectations. So what to believe? Are 40 years of thousands of patients all crazy? Who better to tell us that we are nuts than psychiatrists? They are the best to know. If they tell you this is REAL, one has to pay attention.

If I reject this, what rational reason do I give? Do I simply have a closed mind and cannot handle the truth, pure preconceived ignorance. What, it is not in my belief system, and then what does that mean? NOTHING, ABSOLUTELY NOTHING! How do we learn new things if our minds are closed? Do I reject, out of fear, of what, that we all are eternal? Time to rejoice not fear.

I learned many things at this conference but one thing stands out, that love never dies. There is unconditional strong love, before and after this life here on Earth; and love gives our existence here all meaning and understanding. Without it, we are all nothing, and have nothing. Love spans all space and time across dimensions.

CHAPTER 14

MY GIRL TAKES ME HIGHER and HIGHER

This unexpected turn in our spiritual path to Reincarnation ignited a fire within me to learn more. With a relentless attitude of exploring more into the psychic exercises in order to strengthen my Clairvoyance and Clairaudience, was the next step in our journey. The Clairsentience was always our strong suit. The central concept to me was that these mind muscles need to be exercised to make them stronger. Thus, prior to every meditation, I would always start by opening my Chakras and then do a series of mind focus exercises to strengthen my psychic abilities. Chakra is an Indian word-meaning wheel.

With much practice using many forms of meditation, my spiritual senses were improving: the Clairvoyance and Clairaudience. The Clairsentience was strong from the beginning. Felecia very much likes to communicate by Clairsentience. Several literally amazing experiences started to occur with our connections through meditations and visitations into the Fall of 2019. It became a daily regular routine to do what I call "Alpha Checks," or quickly going into the Alpha Brain State to see if Felecia was present. The Alpha and Theta brain states are basically expanded awareness and higher consciousness. It has been called a doorway to the higher worlds.

When she was not there, the difference was dramatic by Clairsentience detection; like there was NOTHING! At times I would receive a "vibe" a brief strong feeling and thus would Alpha Check. There was a 100% correlation when I received a "vibe" with my girl being present. Wherever I would go, no matter what activity I was doing, she was with me. Not all the time but quite often.

Let me briefly describe my new life with my Felecia. When there is something important to do involving finances, or having some minor surgery she is always with me; no doubt. As I previously mentioned, we go to the cemetery together. However, I don't go to the cemetery often now anymore because she is with me, she is NOT there. When we do go to the cemetery, we kind of laugh about it. I have taken several day trips and she is always with me. Wherever I travel, no matter where it is, Felecia is always with me. She always lets me know she is around with her strong waves of Clairsentience love energy, even during my daily activities like going to the supermarket.

My Felecia is always around the house; especially the family room, kitchen, and the living room. At night we meet in the living room usually after 9:00 PM. Before this time I will go into the living room and do "Alpha Checks" to test if she is around, and there is NOTHING ! As mentioned, when she is not there, it is a very dramatic difference from when my girl is present. At times her Clairsentience is so strong I don't have to go into an altered brain state to detect her. My spiritual senses, my central nervous system, have become very sensitive to her presence. It is such a beautiful merging of our energy. We sit on the living room couch and communicate by Clairsentience. I ask 'yes' and 'no' questions. A 'yes' is a strong Clairsentience blast, and 'no' is simply nothing. I tell her about my day, although she usually knows. Remember they hear and see everything. After Felecia and I communicate for a while I say goodnight and I love you and go to bed.

I would highly recommend the books by Dr. Michael Newton, a world famous psychologist, for several decades, representing thousands of patients, who wrote several best selling books. *The Journey of Souls, The Destiny of Souls,* and others, are a must reading. For he discusses in detail about communication with The Other Side, and what it is all about there, in great detail. Plus numerous other topics like Reincarnation.

A turning point occurred in October 2019. It truly was a major breakthrough. How do you describe a miracle of this nature? I am always reading and researching. My dining room table has numerous stacks of books. Amazon Prime just loved me. Couples holding hands with one in spirit and the other in this basic physical dimension has been documented.

On the evening of October 16, 2019 I felt her around me for at least an hour. I sat on the couch in the living room in my favorite spot. I leaned forward and started to talk to her and I felt her in the room. I asked her to step closer. We always held hands every day, at the dinner table and elsewhere. I said out loud Felecia (I called her Tweek too) "let us hold hands." Immediately I felt a strong Clairsentience response JUST IN BOTH MY HANDS TO MY WRISTS. NOWHERE ELSE IN MY BODY! The waves of energy, warmth and tremors just in my hands were absolute. When I have images or thoughts, or say specific things, there will be a powerful Clairsentience response primarily throughout my whole body. When I ask her to touch my heart, there is a specific Clairsentience response in that anatomical location. We touch energetically. Now with requesting to hold hands there was a very specific Clairsentience response in just my hands nowhere else. This truly validates it was my girl hearing me, listening and being present. Remember on The Other Side it is all them! When we cross over, it is still always us. We never stop being us, whether it is in this dimension or the next one. Their personality and everything that makes them has not changed. It is still their total self. Total consciousness survives what we call death. Death is just the transition or trip to the next dimension of life. Not for one moment does so-called death mean we cease to exist.

There is great intelligence on The Other Side. I could not begin how this made me feel, to hold hands with her. I have now added this to the many ways we communicate. I asked her to hold hands with me that evening about 15 times and every time there was a clear strong response.

Now let us assume I am "nuts"! This was just in my imagination. Just a feel good delirium. I went to bed that night all excited and with high energy. Well, the next morning I go on my computer and there is an email that "blows me away." It was a Holy Shit moment! A Medium we worked with months before who I have not heard from in months sends me an email. I don't use this Medium's name because people have the sacred right to have their privacy protected. Now this Medium is a nurse with the wonderful gifts of Clairvoyance and other ways to communicate with spirit. This email comes from England where she describes to me that Felecia paid her a visit that morning and showed her a wall being taken down and curtains were being opened letting in a beautiful sunrise. Spirit often communicates very effectively with symbols and pictures, plus other forms of communication. In other words, there was a major breakthrough. I was then asked by the Medium "does this resonate with me?" Well, Hell Yes!!! Felecia came to this Medium to tell her we held hands last night. A major wall or obstacle was breached. If one looks at the timing of these events it is truly amazing. We held hands last night, then the next morning Felecia sought out this Medium to tell her. WOW!!! This is truly incredible. This truly validates what happened the night before. I have not heard from or been in any form of communication in months with this Medium. She would have no idea what occurred the night before, with Felecia and I. My girl is so smart. She knew how to add "ironclad" credibility to us holding hands the night before. It made me weep with overwhelming love and emotion. One truly has to be an imbecile in not understanding the powerful synchronicity of this. I am in awe of Felecia's acute intelligence. If this did not occur people would just simply say he is "nuts"; it was his imagination, just fantasy. He is trying to make himself feel good. As I mentioned before, all that "feel good" fantasy nonsense to me, a "hard nosed", analytical, objective, evidence guy is just that, nonsense!

CHAPTER 15

TWO EVENTS THAT WERE TRANSFORMATIONAL

I was in such awe and admiration for what Felecia did with us holding hands but how was I to know she was going to control two events that simply were spiritual love power at its finest. Both events occurred in a span of one week, from the end of October to November 5, 2019. It was a miraculous week. I should never underestimate her desire to connect and influence events. Her love is so powerful. Her will to reach out to me and communicate is so strong.

This miraculous week started with the power going out in the house. The power went out at 1:10 in the morning due to a very strong windstorm. For two days the power was out. I can only write and document what I experienced during this time period, with complete truth and the utmost in analytical, rational, objective thought. My girl comes and visits me in a pattern, she is always there in the mornings, when we have a daily meditation and visitation then also in the evening about 9:00 to 10:00 PM. I always challenge and question; she is never there around 1:00 AM to 5:00 AM. How I know this is because I am up those hours almost every night. Many times my family or close friends will receive an email or text from me during those hours.

The power was out at 1:10 AM ; so I came downstairs and went into the living room about 2:00 AM and sat in my favorite spot on the couch. I took a chance to see if she was there. I did an Alpha Brain State Check and sure enough she was there. I do "Alpha Checks" all the time and when my girl is not there it is dramatic, like there is NOTHING.

As I discussed, when she is present, the Clairsentience surge of energy is very powerful, overwhelming at times. Felecia is never there at 2:00 AM; but on the night that the house had no power, she was present. I said, I love you and goodnight and she responded with a strong Clairsentience surge meaning the same to me. I went upstairs to bed.

Now it is about 10:00 in the morning, and the house and I are freezing. I am doing my daily morning meditation and visitation; we held hands several times. My hands were ICE COLD, LIKE ICICLES. NOW THIS IS WHAT REALLY GOT ME. AFTER HOLDING HANDS, THEY IMMEDIATELY became nice and warm and stayed that way for quite awhile. The only thing I can think of is Clairsentience is the merging of pure energy and her energy warmed my hands. My girl actually warmed my hands up. At times, I still cannot believe it, that I am writing this. However, I only can communicate the truth in a rational, objective, analytical frame of mind as humanly possible as to what happened.

The second event was directly related to the one-year anniversary of her Crossing the Veil on November 5, 2018 to now November 5, 2019. Yes, it is an anniversary for lack of a better word. An anniversary of the most terrible day for us, in this life anyway. I could not believe that one-year had already passed by. If anyone had any lingering doubt about living after this life this next event should erase it.

The anniversary date of November 5th on a Tuesday was an extremely exhausting day from every emotional standpoint. The outpouring of love and support from my family and close friends in phone calls, emails, texts, Face Time was overwhelming. That Tuesday night I looked at my emails and there was a totally unexpected email from again the Medium whom Felecia contacted with the major breakthrough of us holding hands as previously mentioned in the last chapter. It appears

Felecia has a connection of comfort with this woman. Thus, she had contacted her again.

This is a quote from the email I received. "She showed a satin type robe, she was wearing; like a Hollywood glamour type with a tie belt, flowing. She keeps talking about a certain type of flowers, looking like pansies, with a liking towards the purple ones."

In reading this totally unexpected email, I was in shock. I sent a response email to this woman, asking: Why of all days Felecia contacted you on this specific day of her anniversary in Crossing the Veil? What time of day did she contact you? What was the color of the robe? This woman's response email shook me to my core. There was definitely more to this from my beloved Felecia. My girl came to this woman TWO DAYS BEFORE the anniversary on Sunday morning, November 3rd.

"She walked through the kitchen wearing a yellow or cream colored satin robe, it appeared to be pastel with many flowers around her. The flowers, pansies, with purple color and the satin robe made her feel like a dream. However, the Medium said I will send this email off to him straight away. My Felecia said "no, not yet."

On Monday, November 4th Felecia showed up at the hospital where this Medium works and she said "Hi" to Felecia and asked "Can I send the email off now?" She just said "no."

Then the next day on Tuesday, November 5th, my girl's crossing over anniversary, this Medium was in a zoom meeting from 4:30-6:00PM EST and Felecia showed up during this meeting and said "Send it now" so this woman did. In addition, Felecia showed "a floral bouquet with a variety of colors, not roses, something else but light like a peony when it first blooms."

This woman said to me in this response email how she was in awe in that Felecia was so certain she wanted her to wait to send this email to me. She was in total awe on how communication with our loved ones can be.

When I received this return email from this woman I was in total astonishment.

Felecia had her wait TWO DAYS, from Sunday, November 3rd, to Tuesday, November 5th, before the email was to be sent to me. My Felecia had her wait the two days so I would receive it on the one-year anniversary of November 5th. I was in total amazement. She wanted to make sure I received that email on the one-year anniversary. This was not random by my Felecia. She actually PLANNED that the message be sent on Tuesday. The mere fact that she waited for the message to be sent on the anniversary validates everything since THIS MEDIUM HAD NO IDEA OF THE SIGNIFICANCE OF TUESDAY. Felecia's message was simple, basically saying I AM ALIVE AND WELL. I still exist. I did NOT die!!!

Separation between my girl and I is an illusion.

Anyone with a rational mind, after this sequence of events, would have to say Felecia is really alive and well; not as wishful thinking nor hope nor faith but as FACT. It is so rationally powerful that it is actually irrational not to accept this as fact!

CHAPTER 16

A NEW DIRECTION IN OUR JOURNEY: TARGET CLAIRSENTIENCE

Love is such a beautiful thing. It picks you up no matter how many times you fall. Love is the only thing that is real. Her love is within me, part of my total being. The new direction in our Spiritual Journey was starting to take shape and it involved a much closer look at Reincarnation and obtaining information on The Other Side. Plus, a more advanced degree of Clairsentience, coupled with Clairvoyance was evolving at a rapid pace.

What inspired me to take these directions was not only the past events in Seattle with the EMDR therapy, and the week with Dr. Brian Weiss at the Omega Institute, but in addition the books by Dr. Michael Newton. Dr. Newton is a world famous psychologist, who not only had extensive clinical experience for decades with Past Lives Regression Therapy but also what is called LBL, Life Between Lives. In other words, we spend a fraction of our existence here in this basic physical realm whereas most of our existence is on The Other Side or The Spirit World. So what is it like on The Other Side? What do we do there?

Now a very important concept stated by Dr. Newton was all his patients for several decades while under hypnosis, there was an absolute consistency of what The Spirit World was like. It DID NOT MATTER if the person was an atheist, a deeply religious individual, nor any other culture or philosophy. The testimonials were all the same, very consistent over several decades of research.

People may have images of spirits sitting on clouds, in the mist, with harps playing. In many respects it is more active than here with a higher sense of reality and consciousness. On The Other Side spirits don't require sleep and don't need to eat. We are "Time Bound" on This Side but on The Other Side there is no time, there is eternity. It is stated you are in The NOW OF GOD. Everything happens in The Now. You don't get old, there are no seasons, there is no sun to rise and set as barometers of time. There is a constant very comfortable 72 degrees with a beautiful softly bright sky that is soul nourishing. In many respects their energy bodies, which is a mirror image, of the one here is more physical and solid than here. There is ground to walk on; walls that can be touched and buildings to reside in. Their hearts beat and they breathe. There is a vast array of activities and work projects. There is no money so everything is done to help each other. Plus, the Spirit World is a place of humor, socializing, and fun. Now to get your attention let's talk sex. It is not like here but it is called MERGING. A total blending in every aspect: physically, spiritually, and emotionally. It is described as a state of total bliss and extraordinarily intense.

My Felecia and I were advancing so fast in our many connections through meditations and visitations, and during my daily activities, that now the stage was set for information gathering on our Past Lives Together and The Other Side. Who better to ask what it is like on The Other Side, and specific information about us, than my Felecia? The information obtained comes from several months of twice daily meditations and visitations in the morning and at night with Felecia. After the November 5th anniversary of my girl Crossing the Veil, our daily routine was of this nature. I would wake up in the morning and start my Mind Focus Exercises by first opening up my Chakras. Then concentrating on practice to strengthen my Clairvoyance (to see) through the Minds' Eye, also called the Third Eye or 6th Chakra and Clairaudience (to hear or better to listen).

In my meditations to strengthen my Clairvoyance, one exercise is to visualize a symbol, a word or number in your mind's eye. Immediately when I started to practice this specific Clairvoyance exercise appeared two symbols. The first one was of a triangle and the second one was of infinity. In brief, my research told me what these two symbols meant from a spiritual viewpoint. The triangle is the strongest shape, it represents strength. It can also symbolize love, truth and wisdom. Now the infinity symbol represents related to love: eternity and everlasting love. To my surprise, these symbols out of nowhere immediately appeared in my mind's eye or third eye. Of all the words, numbers, symbols in the universe these two appeared instantly. I found the instant appearance of these two symbols and their spiritual meanings a very interesting synchronicity. As if the Spirit World was trying to tell me something.

I look upon this in a simplistic way that these are psychic Mind Muscles that the more you use them the stronger they become. In many respects one is opening neural pathways that have hardly been used. A greater use and activation of the right hemisphere of the brain. This requires lots of discipline, practice, perseverance, patience, focus and "a never give up attitude." As I said previously my motto is simply "Never Give Up, Just Keep On Going." It does not matter how many times you fall, it is getting up that counts.

The Clairsentience is very strong between Felecia and I, so that was not an issue. My central nervous system has become so sensitive to my girl's presence. In all of my life nothing has come close to the experience of Clairsentience.

After these Mind Focus exercises I was ready for a meditation and visitation with Felecia. I use many forms or techniques of meditation. I would always start with a prayer to Source, God, or OM, whichever word one prefers for guidance and protection and to ask both our Spirit Guides (advisors) and angels to help us with a wonderful connection of communion. The place for the meditation was, when I was home, either in the dining room or living room. When I was on the road I would always find a quiet place to shut out the world. She is always immediately ready to make the connection no matter what form of meditation I use. My girl's desire to communicate is overwhelming. She is a woman on a mission of great determination and love. Our love will never be denied.

There were a number of times that if I was doing some other activity first in the morning before our meditation visits she would smack me in the face with her beautiful, mild, sweet, soft perfume several times to get my attention; as if to say "Hey let's visit!" No delays here. My girl is so funny and amazing at the same time. BRAVO, BRAVO! They simply don't get any better than her. After the prayer and asking for assistance from both our angels and Spirit Guides then Felecia and I would have a wonderful connection of the communion of love; we would establish a strong Clairsentience bond. How this was performed was we would blend our energy in many different ways. Every morning became an exhilarating experience of connection.

When I would ask her to MERGE WITHIN ME either out loud or by thought, with the image in my mind of her walking towards me and merging within me, I would receive such a "blast" of energy throughout my whole body. The energy would actually travel through my whole body down to my fingertips. My fingertips would actually vibrate. I only could say WOW! There is nothing like it. I have gained so much respect for the power of thought. THOUGHT RULES on The Other Side and throughout the universe. This is my favorite Clairsentience connection; it is like being in the power together. People don't realize our loved ones are just a thought away. People need to own their power. Energy has no limits, no boundaries. The infusion of energy into ones' physical being is beyond description. One is actually closer to a loved one now than in the physical realm because they are closer to your mind, heart and physical being. People simply have no idea what they are missing. People need to own their own power.

I would then say again, either out loud or by thought, A TOTAL BLENDING OF OUR BEING and have that image of our total energy bodies infusing together. Like two beautiful glowing white lights merging together. There was then a huge burst of white light outward, a supernova of love light. The energy result was an incredible feeling.

Then I would ask Felecia TO TOUCH MY HEART and would have the image of a beam of light directly going to my heart space and I would feel the Clairsentience energy just in that location to my heart. It was highly focused.

When I would ask my girl for a HUG I would only receive a strong Clairsentience response just in my central chest area. Finally, throughout a meditation I always would say out loud or sometimes by thought to please HOLD MY HANDS or at times I would say squeeze my hands. I then would only receive a powerful Clairsentience energy response just in my hands to my wrists and nowhere else in my body. At times we would hold ONE HAND OR TWO. Also, I would just stretch out my arms with the hand palms up and I would feel Clairsentience waves up my hands traveling up both arms. I started to call all these different feelings of focused energy TARGET CLAIRSENTIENCE that I will describe later in detail.

At this point I would start to ask my eternal love questions. When I would ask Felecia a question a Clairsentience Blast was a yes and a no was nothing! There was no doubt in the answer received. Plus, in my mind's eye, numbers and letters, words would form and would take on a solid nature in my mind. The information she would send me was immediate after a question asked and very clear. When I received numbers or letters making up dates, words and names I would ask her out loud is this what you mean? The information was then repeated. She would confirm it with a Clairsentience blast as a yes or no. Many times words, names were spelled out. Letters, words, and numbers appeared in my mind's eye by Clairvoyance and confirmed by Clairsentience. Answers were achieved by two methods. At times unexpectedly, my girl would float numbers by me being dates, in my mind's eye without me asking a question. Then I would start asking all kinds of questions. Over weeks I would confirm and reconfirm information many times. Trying to be as accurate and careful of the information received. I was always testing, confirming, reconfirming, double, triple checking. Looking for complete consistency. That is just the medicine and science guy in me. I guess it just is in my DNA.

In addition to our meditation visits my girl would come at times during the day if I needed support or accompany me on my daily activities. However, many times she goes away related to her activities on The Other Side. Our days and nights became structured with morning and nighttime visits which I will describe in more detail later. I realized, through all of this, that our communication was so constant and extensive every day that we did not need a Medium to communicate. I was like a ONE SPIRIT MEDIUM! Now the stage was set for the asking of questions to my very beautiful Felecia.

CHAPTER 17

OUR REAL ETERNAL NAMES and THE SOUL LEARNING CURVE

A guidance for me were the numerous books by Dr. Michael Newton on critical information obtained over several decades with many thousands of patients. These books are truly a compendium of guidance and information on The Other Side.

One of the first questions that came up after reading his books was I noticed that every soul on The Other Side has an Eternal Spiritual Name. We all have names in every past life specific for that particular life. It would get very confusing since there were so many names associated with so many lives. However, the name that NEVER CHANGES is our name on The Other Side. It is our Eternal Name, Our Real Name that is consistent through all lives and eternity.

In one of our morning meditations one of the first questions I asked Felecia was what was my spiritual name or soul name on The Other Side? The answer came back immediately and very clear. The letters were clear and I spelled it out to confirm. What came through was URA. This was confirmed several times in subsequent meditations. At first when I heard Ura, I laughed. I never heard of this word or name. First, was it an actual word? The next day, as curiosity got the better of me, I researched Ura on the computer. I was blown away as far as the information that was revealed. If one looks at the research of URA, these letters are a word, it is an actual word and plus a real name. It can be either a name for a girl or boy. If one looks at one of the very ancient languages of the world is Sanskrit in India.

Sanskrit can be traced back to at least 2000 BC, over four thousand years ago. The name URA means LOVED FROM THE HEART. Is that appropriate or what? This was impossible for me to know. These letters that appeared in my mind's eye, my Clairvoyance, was not only a real word but also an actual ancient language first name meaning LOVED FROM THE HEART. This was an epiphany moment. I could not fake this if I tried. I would not know how to fake this. Felecia confirmed this several times in subsequent meditations. There is no conceivable way that I would know of this name and language. The only rational explanation is that it came from my Felecia.

A few days later I asked Felecia what was her eternal or spiritual name on The Other Side in one of our daily meditations? Immediately and clearly she responded to me spelling out the letters KLEA. Again, I researched KLEA and again not only these letters were an actual word but also a female name in ancient Greek meaning GLORY, FAMOUS, A PROUD NAME. This was very appropriate to say the least. So where did this come from? Certainly not from me. Obviously, the only rational explanation was it came from my Felecia. Both these names are ancient in origin and I absolutely had no clue of their existence. Thus, our Real Spiritual Eternal Names on The Other Side are KLEA and URA. It makes sense to have that continuity of one name because it would be very confusing having so many other names corresponding to all our past lives.

I noticed too in my readings of Newton's massive information base that souls on The Other Side have nicknames in their Soul Group. After numerous meditations and confirmed several times Klea's nickname is TILA and Ura's is CRIG. I asked Klea why I am called Crig in our Soul Group because I am funny. I asked Klea why in the Soul Pack she is called TILA; and she tells me because she is pretty. Now that is a gross understatement. Not because she is my Klea but Mediums have stated to me when she came for a visit that quote "she is gorgeous." In the Spirit World physical beauty is a mark of an elevated soul. That certainly is my girl! On The Other Side we return to an age of our choosing. My Klea decided to return to the age of about 25.

There is extensive information from Michael Newton's research, and others that is quite interesting in that souls run in groups or packs. They are called Spirit Groups or Packs. These souls stay together from their inception into existence for all eternity. They are at approximately the same level of advancement on the soul learning curve. After the transition back to The Other Side by so-called death, we return to our Soul Group where we recognize those souls who we have been reincarnating with us for eons. In order to experience all the different types of love, members of a Soul Group will exchange their family or friend roles. For instance, souls can be your mother and father in one life then in other lives your sons and daughters.

The Soul Group moves forward together. It is all about the evolution, improvement, betterment of the soul during and after the numerous incarnations to Earth and other worlds. Another way to put it is the purpose of life is for the soul to learn lessons to enhance and advance the spirituality of the soul. The incarnations increase your purity of spirit. Earth is considered a very difficult school because a soul has both mental and physical challenges here. The spirituality of the soul is the central theme. It is like having eternal classmates who help each other. There is an innermost group of souls up to 5. With this inner group one is most intimate for all eternity. The primary Soul Group is then up to about 30. After that, one gets into community Soul Groups that can be up to 1,000 souls and other large groups. After several meditations with confirmations, the size of the Soul Group Klea and Ura are in is 20. I asked her through many meditations, all kinds of numbers when I asked 20 souls in our group I received a huge Clairsentience yes response many times.

Now a central issue is why do souls incarnate into a human body? There is an immense amount of information on this question from countless sources. In brief, it is all about the evolution of the soul, the improvement of the soul in learning lessons that can ONLY be learned in the physical form. We are Interdimensional Spirit Beings (ISB) that take on human form to learn. NOT human beings having a spiritual experience. That is a major difference. Our true essence is not physical.

The soul learns about all of the different manifestations of love, compassion, forgiveness, and gratitude. As an example, in one incarnation a soul may have to learn about a specific type of love, compassion, gratitude or forgiveness and yes, pain. Some of the best lessons are learned through pain. In the advancement of the soul there are lessons to learn, debts to pay from past lives, karma at work.

Your eternal Soul Group classmates are approximately at the same point on the learning curve. My own viewpoint about these multiple incarnations related to God or Source (OM) is that all souls are particles of energy from Source. In other words, we have God in all of us. Source is perfection. A soul starts out imperfect and through the eons of time, by all these incarnations, strives for improvement of the spiritual nature to become closer to perfect; and to strive for perfection in the image of Source. Do souls ever attain perfection? I have no idea. It is a sacred spiritual circle. A soul begins its journey of imperfection and through the process of incarnations and life in the Spirit World strives in its evolution for perfection. The spiritual circle closes and is complete.

If one reads Newton's books, there is information that was collected and achieved over decades about the characteristics of the learning curve itself. Where you are as a soul on the learning curve is related to the colors of your core soul energy on The Other Side. Plus, there are colors in a halo around souls that signifies traits of that specific soul. This is different from the colors of the Aura that people have on Earth here in physical form. It is like in Karate one has colors on their belt to indicate where they are on the learning curve of that discipline.

In general, the classification of the development of the spiritual maturity of souls is like this: There are beginners with solid White (Level 1) and Intermediate with solid Yellow (Level 3) and finally very advanced souls with light Blue (Level 5). There are color variations in between each level. Furthermore, as mentioned there are colors in a halo around souls on The Other Side which gives the trait characteristics such as attitudes, beliefs of that soul.

After numerous meditations in confirmation of asking Klea what were the colors of our core soul energy; the bottom line was that we are both in The Intermediate Level 3 with solid yellow. In accordance with Newton's massive database this indicates attributes of being Protective, Strength, and Courage. Again, after numerous meditations I asked my girl what were the halo colors around the solid yellow soul core color? Again she told me, after several confirmations, green and purple are the colors of our halo surrounding the core yellow. Now according to Newton's classification that signifies characteristics of: Green = Healing, Nurturing, and Compassion; Purple = Wisdom, Truth, and Divinity. Well, this certainly fits my Klea, who had all these traits in abundance. For me, I will wait to see when I Cross the Veil and return HOME.

CHAPTER 18

KLEA and URA: THE DAYS OF OUR PAST LIVES THROUGH ETERNITY

In September after the conference at the Omega Institute I had numerous vivid detailed constant memories of several past lives in my daily meditations before and especially after the conference. The dominant one was about 200 - 300 BC in Rome, but also 11th Century Mongolia and 17th Century England. My Klea was not only with me in life in ancient Rome but also in 17th Century England.

The memories intensified. The memories in my meditations would repeat constantly, with greater and more vivid detail, with especially color and moments of great emotion. The thesis is that memories are being slowly released from the subconscious mind to the conscious mind as a function of time. For Klea, the understanding is once one Crosses the Veil, the amnesia blocks are released and information is revealed about all the past lives of a soul. The answers are in the past. When we cross over, memories of our past lives come flooding back, unblocked. There is a unification of the conscious and subconscious minds. Plus, we use a higher degree of our mind on The Other Side, in comparison to This Side. My beautiful Klea will have much information to share with me. In addition, as I will explain later, there is a Hall of Records on The Other Side where every conceivable aspect of information in the universe is stored.

Information was primarily transmitted two ways, by Clairvoyance (to see) and Clairsentience (to feel). In addition to that, at times by Clairaudience (to hear or better to listen). In my mind's eye the Clairvoyance was no doubt. With confirmation by her powerful Clairsentience response, when I asked follow up questions. Information was then confirmed and reconfirmed several times. There was much double-checking. Many times, I would receive information and then let several days pass, and return to confirm the information to look for consistency. Numerous times, the numbers and letters took on a three dimensional form, as being solid in my mind's eye.

I was astonished, to say the least what my Klea was telling me. I only can tell the truth as humanly possible from a rational, objective and analytical standpoint. Over the course of several months, and numerous daily morning and evening meditations, much more information surfaced from Klea about our past lives together.

We set up a CHART of REINCARNATION. It will NEVER be complete. The information will not be ultimately verified and become absolute, until I Cross the Veil. This shows the numerous millennia of our past lives together. Furthermore, keep in mind this is just the lives of Klea and Ura being together. There are other past lives in which we were not together as a couple.

Presented is the information on the many past lives Klea and Ura have been together through several thousands of years into the Stone Age.

Across the travails of time we had many names, guises and faces, through many battles and tribulations. However, through it all, across time and space, it was us, still us!

CHART OF REINCARNATION for KLEA and URA

PRESENT	Felecia and Leonard – **New York, USA** – two sons
1903 AD	**Italy,** Angelina and Emilio – lived in the village of Sant'Angelo di Piove di Sacco – two children – one son and one daughter
1806 AD	**Ship at sea** (Atlantic Ocean) - Toby and Kenneth, on route from Ireland to America....Just married, we were so young, no children.....Perished at sea
1736 AD	**England** – Clare and Benjamin – had one child...a daughter
1642 AD	**Germany** – Safha and Tandel – had three children – three daughters
1541 AD	**Spain** – (The Renaissance) – Ana and Franco – had two children – one son and one daughter
703 AD	**Lithuania** (before it was Lithuania) Myrath and Raj – had five children – one still born – three daughters and one son
535 AD	**Honduras** (before it was called Honduras, in Central America) – Rotta and Tiko – had five children – four sons and one daughter
135 AD	**Mesopotamia –** Atta and Vebra – had three sons – Mesopotamia was an ancient region in the Eastern Mediterranean Sea, bordered by the Zagros Mountains in the northeast, composed of mostly present day Iraq, but also Turkey, Iran, and Syria
207 BC	**Rome, Italy** - Antonia and Claudius – two children – one son and one daughter
1038 BC	**Crimean Peninsula** in the Black Sea (Ukraine, before the name Crimea) – Tika and Noak had six children – three sons and three daughters
3016 BC	**Ancient Egypt –** Mira and Ptolemy – had four children – three sons and one daughter
5050 BC	**Samara Civilization (5th Millennium BC, Upper Volga River, Russia) –** Ena and Farouk – six children – four daughters and two sons

Three Past Lives In The Stone Age

7543 BC	Neolithic Period or New Stone Age
10009 BC	Cusp of the Paleolithic, Old Stone Age and Mesolithic, Middle Stone Age
15043 BC	The Old Stone Age, our first life together here

There were three lives that Klea and Ura shared in the Stone Age before 5050 BC. The Stone Age has three periods: the Paleolithic or Old Stone Age from 30,000 to 10,000 BC, Mesolithic or Middle Stone Age from 10,000 to 8,000 BC, and the Neolithic or New Stone Age from 8,000 to 3,000 BC. Through my Clairvoyance, and confirmed several times by Clairsentience, my Klea gave me the following dates: 15043 BC, 10009 BC, and 7543 BC for the three past lives we shared in the Stone Age. The first life we shared was in 15043 BC, The Old Stone Age, which means Klea and Ura have been together for over 17,000 years. Which also means our souls came into existence greater than 17,000 years ago. Described another way, our souls are older than 17,000 years. The next past life we shared was in 10009 BC which is on the cusp of the Paleolithic, Old Stone Age and Mesolithic, Middle Stone Age Periods. The third past life in the Stone Age was in 7543 BC which was in the Neolithic Period or the New Stone Age. My Klea told me she made visits to the Hall of Records several times to confirm all of this, which I will discuss later. I did not ask about our names because during those time periods we most likely just grunted at each other. Klea also confirmed several times to me that we had no children in these three past lives in the Stone Age.

My mind just got overloaded with all this incredible information. I needed to take a break and a breather for awhile. I tried to be as humanly careful as possible in obtaining this information. I was always questioning, confirming, and reconfirming, over months. I was always double checking everything, looking for consistency. It would be literally impossible for me to know any of this information. I would not know where to begin. I would not know how to fake, make this stuff up if I tried. There were names and world locations I never heard of!

What I found very interesting in speculation was the meanings of some of these names. Some of these names were quite ancient, from the very ancient language Sanskrit. Here are a few examples:

- **Angelina** = Angel, messenger of God
- **Myrath** = Legacy
- **Antonia** = Priceless
- **Raj** = King/rule
- **Ptolemy** = Aggressive, Warlike
- **Farouk** = Seer of Truth
- **Tandel** = Captain of the Ship

Just some interesting speculation. What I found quite profound is that the names for both of us reflected the time periods, world locations, cultures, and several civilizations of the world. As examples, you don't see names like Susan, John or Carol in ancient Egypt, Honduras, Crimea, Mesopotamia, Lithuania, and elsewhere. Compelling were the dates that my Klea gave me had corresponded, in every case, to the time period of these civilizations. I would not know how to begin to do this.

Notice this Reincarnation History goes across all races, ethnic, religious groups, creeds, and nationalities. Bigotry, prejudice are man made concepts here on THIS SIDE, NOT ON THE OTHER SIDE. In the history of our past lives we know about we were: Italians, Irish, English, Germans, Spanish, ancient Lithuanians, Hondurans, Mesopotamians, Romans, Crimeans, Egyptians, and Samaritans. "Heaven Knows" what we were in the three lives in the Stone Age. It is recognized that we are connected souls all to each other. We are part of the universal collective consciousness. We are ONE with each other and with Source, who is in all of us. We are ONE in the brotherhood and sisterhood of love.

The Clairvoyance to see, the Clairaudience to hear and the Clairsentience to feel, and combinations of these insights, all started with the images of the past life experience in Ancient Rome with my Klea, while under EMDR therapy in Seattle, WA. These images continued for several months. At times, for some unexplained reason, memories in the subconscious mind will surface from a distant past life and not from recent past lives. Prior to that experience in Seattle, there never was any thought or interest in Reincarnation. It simply never occurred to me. I never gave it much thought. Reincarnation was just a word to me. I CANNOT OVER EMPHASIZE THE FACT THAT WHEN THIS SPIRITUAL JOURNEY BEGAN I WAS THE ULTIMATE SKEPTIC.

During the time period after Seattle, I had repeating vivid, emotional, detailed images not only in Ancient Rome, but also 17th Century England, and 11th Century Mongolia, in my meditations. My Klea was dominant in Ancient Rome as mentioned but also in 17th Century England. In the past life of 11th Century Mongolia, she was not present.

Afterwards, in our meditations, I started to ask questions about our past life in 17th Century England. For some unexplained reason for all the other past lives there were no images at all. One of the mysteries of the mind.

Of great interest, later on detailed images started to develop in one of our daily morning meditations of us together on a ship at sea with very vivid colors. These images lasted for weeks. My Klea was in a light blue bonnet hat and matching fluffy dress for that time period, that culture, and that location of the world, Ireland. She was a vision of beauty. I was in a dark Gentlemen's Suit. We were just married and filled with such hopes and dreams for a life together in America. She was my beautiful Toby and I was her Kenneth. We were so young and deeply in love. I could see lots and lots of water. This past life in 1806 would end suddenly and tragically with us perishing at sea on our voyage to America.

The images that I could see with us together were only in three past lives, Ancient Rome, 17th Century England, and 1806 on a ship at sea sailing for America. All the other past lives there were no images. I also noticed our past lives were across race, nationality, and ethnic groups. There is no bigotry, prejudice on The Other Side. That is a human trait here on This Side.

This is all about the eternal cycles of the soul for the evolution of spiritual development and improvement. The sad thing is people today have minimal or no connection to their real self, the soul. People simply don't have a clue as to what and who they really are. We are eternally linked to our past. We are our past. Past lives can give us greater understanding of the life we are living now. The more we learn about our past lives, the more sense our current life makes. What we are is eternal Interdimensional Spirit Beings (ISB) having human experiences in order to advance the spirituality of our soul. We take on human form to accomplish this. With all the different ways my Klea and I communicate we now developed a daily spiritual communication routine.

PICTURES OF OUR PRESENT LIFE

The Angel and I are attending a Halloween Hospital Party

Our First Wedding Anniversary

Attending a 1950's and 1960's Party

A later years Wedding Anniversary with the two birds on the cake.

Our Wedding Cake Top

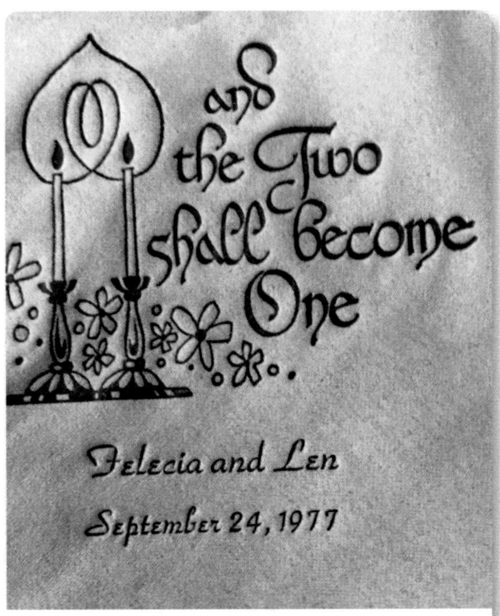

We became ONE that day

Felecia (KLEA) collected and gave me the LOVE IS captions from the newspaper

The end of the many parties at Grandmas house in the Bronx. I'm the kid with the bread in hand and short pants "hanging out" with some of the guys.

CHAPTER 19

OUR SPIRITUAL JOURNEY DEVELOPS A DAILY ROUTINE

My Klea and I were progressing so fast. It was like every few days there was a new revelation. Our daily routine that developed would start when I would wake up about 7:30 to 8:00 AM in the morning. The first thing I would do is my initial mind focus exercises by opening my Chakras. As previously mentioned the opening of the Chakras enhance and strengthen psychic and intuitive abilities. Then I would practice mind focus exercises on strengthening my Clairaudience, to hear or listen and Clairvoyance, to see. In my view, I look upon it as simply mind muscles, the more one uses them the stronger they become. You are opening neural pathways that have not been used. It is always important to remember the right hemisphere of the brain, which is responsible for intuition, creativity, psychic properties, insight, and imagination. The ever-present Clairsentience for us is always there and very strong. It was our strong suit right from the beginning. The gift of Clairsentience was a blessing from God to us.

At this point I am ready to start my meditation and visitation with my girl. I use many forms of meditation techniques. She is there immediately and very strong and powerful by Clairsentience, to feel. My Klea is present 100% of the time she never lets me down. My girl is always ready to connect. It is all about the will to communicate and connect on both sides. Communication is always a two way street. Powerful waves of pure spirit energy of love are ever present. Klea's energy of love is now within me. Her love now is part of my very being.

The Spirit World is just as physical as our world but has a different nature. It is on a much higher energy vibration frequency. The matter is actually denser than our realm here. Just above what most people's senses can perceive. The laws of physics are different. You just have to find the right frequency like tuning in on a radio. One just has to turn the dial in meditation. In meditation we raise our vibration levels. It is a meeting of vibration frequencies, termed "The Quickening".

Our culture is so caught up in the "hustle and bustle" that most are not tuned in to the subtle presence of spirit that surrounds all of us. We are just so preoccupied; that we miss so much that we can feel, hear, and see. People fall into the trap that if they cannot detect something with their crude five senses it does not exist. The physical world here on Earth is a very limited collection of vibrations in the universe. The most powerful energy in this spiritual universe of ours is love. In our spiritual connection of Clairsentience, Clairvoyance, and Clairaudience, we communicate. In these meditations, information has been transmitted to me about the numerous past lives we have shared together down through the many thousands of years into the Stone Age.

Every morning, it is such an exhilarating experience of communication. I never experienced anything like it in my entire life. My central nervous system has become so sensitive to her presence. Many times even before we start a meditation; a visit, I start to feel her presence around me with very subtle vibrations. Then when we start the meditation the energy vibrations dramatically increase in power and we start "rocking and rolling." As I use the expression sometimes "hold onto your butts!"

About 8:30-9:00 AM, I have my breakfast. Klea sits at the breakfast table with me. We hold hands. We always had our morning cup of coffee together so I still pour her a cup of coffee with me. My girl calls it the "loving cup." Remember they hear and see everything. Many times now my Dad has been coming. He smacks me several times in the face with the smell of his cigars as one of his favorite songs is playing on the TV's Easy Listening Channel. My Clairvoyance has greatly improved; so I can see them. I measure the accuracy of my Clairvoyance by describing the clothes and jewelry she is wearing. Many times she simply puts her arm around my shoulder. I see it and at times I feel it. She tells me if I am right by a Clairsentience response. My accuracy is running about 80%. My beautiful Klea many times will get my attention with her mild, soft, beautiful perfume. It is so much more pleasant than my Dad smacking me in the face with the smell of his cigar smoke.

Now during the day my girl will come if something has occurred in which she can support me. However, she goes away at times tending to her activities on The Other Side. I could do all the "Alpha Checks" and meditations that I want, till I "Knock myself out" but if she is NOT present then there is NOTHING!!! I could stand on my head and there would be nothing.

My Klea is ALWAYS at ALL family functions "big time" and she is very active. Family was everything to my girl. When I am traveling such as at an airport I will do an "Alpha Check" and she will be there with me. Klea will give me a few target Clairsentience blasts and then there is no doubt. Whether I am in crowds or not has no effect. I can be sitting on an airplane in my seat and before we take off, sometimes I will "Alpha Check" and sure enough she is there. Many times I will ask her, you are sitting next to me aren't you?; "Bingo" I get a strong Clairsentience yes, and we both laugh. Numerous times I am sitting in a restaurant with friends or alone and I "Alpha Check" and my girl never lets me down. My Clairvoyance gives me a very accurate assessment in locating her, and what she is wearing in clothes and jewelry and I confirm everything by Clairsentience. I can be sitting in a meditation room waiting for a therapeutic massage and bingo Klea is there big time.

As I mentioned earlier in the book my girl was a phenomenal cook with everything but especially Italian food. I am in our kitchen attempting to make a Marinara sauce, which is meatless, with angel hair pasta. I could sense she was with me so I did an "Alpha Check" and sure enough she was standing right next to me. I detected she was laughing at my attempt at being a cook. The location, activity, and the people I am with have no effect on our connecting. Nothing will stop us from communicating and being together. The Veil will never stop us. Nothing will ever deny us from being together. The bond between us transcends the different dimensions.

At our home I will be rearranging things and she is right there with me. For example, one day I was cleaning up and rearranging the "sideboard or breakfront" in the dining room. I placed her beautiful wedding picture in the middle, and on the sides I placed more wedding pictures of her with the top to our wedding cake. When I was finished I asked her out loud if she approved or liked what I did; not doing an "Alpha Check" and she immediately gave me her Clairsentience blast approval. She follows me around the house and I can pick her up by gentle "vibes" I feel. I can be cleaning the upstairs bathroom and I can sense she is right behind me. Many times, during our meditations later I confirm what happened during the day with her around.

My girl then shows up in the evenings around 9:00 PM, not before. As I often do "Alpha Checks" and she usually is not there before 8:00 PM. We sit on the living room couch and communicate. At first, I said goodnight to my Klea, told her I loved her, and went upstairs to our bed. Never thinking that she would be following me upstairs and laying in bed next to me. Then, one night it was about 3:00 AM in the morning and I was awake just laying in bed thinking. Then all of a sudden to get my attention she is smacking me several times in the face with her perfume. Basically saying to me, hey "dummy" I am laying right next to you. As I mentioned before sometimes I can be dense and miss things.

Now after we communicate on the living room couch we then go upstairs to bed. I mentioned how Klea and I do Target Clairsentience with holding hands, hugs, a blending of our total being, touching my heart, and her merging within me. We added one more activity to the menu as she targets her Clairsentience energy just in specific locations as I ask her. One night in our communication in the living room I asked my girl when we go upstairs tonight let's spoon as we did when she was here in this physical form in this basic realm. Thus, when we got in bed I turned on my right side and said honey let's spoon all of a sudden I received a powerful Clairsentience blast just in my back, my whole back, nowhere else. Every time I said, "let's spoon" a blast occurred. I was so amazed I was yelling out loud it works, it works! We both laughed. Now many nights we have a "Clairsentience Spoon" as an expression of our deep eternal love and affection. The veil will never stop the expression of our love and communication.

Something else occurred on Valentine's Day 2020, which was on a Friday. For about a month I kept asking my Klea if we would have our first kiss. Her response was always, yes, but it never occurred till the night of Valentine's Day, when decades before we got engaged. Well, I asked again the night of Valentine's Day in bed and sure enough I felt just on my face soft gentle waves of energy. Just on my face nowhere else. My Klea waited till Valentine's Day for this very special expression of love and affection. I now call this our ENERGY KISS! We are getting really good at kissing. Considering when she was here in this basic physical realm we always were great kissers. My girl actually wore red for Valentine's Day as determined by seeing with my subjective Clairvoyance. She confirmed it with a Clairsentience strong yes. Everything that is determined through Clairvoyance and at times Clairaudience I confirm with Clairsentience. She always continues to amaze me and keeps me in awe of her.

Let me add one thing regarding when she is not there, and I cannot pick her up by Clairsentience when I do "Alpha Checks." Remember the Spirit World hears and sees everything in this basic physical dimension. The Spirit World is right here, "Hiding in Plain Sight." These dimensions are very close. Their higher energy dimension is practically right on top of us. One night it was about 1:30 AM in the morning and I was sick. I took a chance and called out to her. At first my Klea was not there by my "Alpha Checks." However, within moments she was there "big time" by her Clairsentience presence. She came fast! There were other times when at the approximate moments in the morning of 5:30 AM I was getting "flashbacks," simply horrible images of her last moments here. As mentioned, she Crossed the Veil at 5:31 AM. I would call out to her because the images of her last moments were pure anguish, pain and suffering deep within my soul. I could not take it! She was there immediately on those nights to comfort me. Thankfully, those images ceased in occurrence. So I asked her several times that although you are NOT right here, you are close by to hear me and immediately come to comfort me if I need you. Her answer to me every time is she is close by. Keep in mind The Other Side is right here among us, another dimension superimposed on our own world here. There is only a thin veil of higher energy vibration frequencies separating us. That is the only thing that separates HERE from THERE. Thus, although I cannot pick her up when I do "Alpha Checks" she is within hearing distance and close by, when I need her. Distance, time, and space have different meanings in the Spirit World and other dimensions because the laws of physics are very different. My girl is simply the best.

Let me explain somewhat about the concept of time. As I have mentioned the laws of physics are different between these dimensions. Our concept of time does not exist on The Other Side. Time in our physical realm here is linear: past, present, and future. On The Other Side as Einstein stated, "There is no time." Past, present, and future are together, in other words everything is NOW. Time literally just about stops on The

Other Side. If 100 years goes by here, it is just a moment on The Other Side. Thus, when we undertake a life, an incarnation here, having a long full life, on The Other Side we are gone for about an "overnight" or less. In other words, The Other Side is a "timeless" dimension for all eternity.

Our time in bed together I now call our "Interdimensional Pillow Talk." Including our Clairsentience affection we discuss various things. I said to her after the continual development of our past lives I said you know we had a lot of "kids" in our previous lives; we laughed. The next morning she tells me in our meditation and visitation the total is 38 children. Whew, I was impressed. Through the many thousands of years, it was a glorious copulation across time and space! We talked about the many weddings and times we got married, again and again. We actually do laugh often together. We are a great comedy team. We also discussed in our Pillow Talk that there were lives in which we died young in the many thousands of years we shared numerous lives.

Months later, after the development of The Reincarnation Chart, I decided to ask my Klea if she could go to the Hall of Records, which I will explain later, and find out what our total incarnations were for both of us. The next day in meditations she told me, 61 incarnations for me and 57 for her excluding this present life. Thus, if you include this present life, the total number of incarnations for Klea and myself were 58 and 62, respectively. WOW, when I Cross the Veil and return HOME, I am staying on The Other Side. I am done. I will exercise my right of free will, which is one of the laws of the universe. This will be my last incarnation!

I laugh because we discussed how she at times looks over my shoulder as I am writing this book. Many times I feel her presence over my shoulder. She tells me that on The Other Side I am an advanced teacher which is considered a position of respected standing. This makes sense because in this life, I taught across the USA and all over the world, various medical audiences, on the aspects of Infectious Diseases. Every day and night is exciting, exhilarating, and simply amazing with my Klea. I never dreamed in any capacity the remaining years of my life, in this specific life, in this basic physical realm would be something of this nature. In all these previous chapters of this book there has been much discussion of so many experiences, information and evidence of the Spiritual Journey of love of Klea and Ura. I now relish and look forward to discussing THE SKEPTIC.

CHAPTER 20

THE SKEPTIC

I devoted a complete chapter to The Skeptic, because once one carefully examines all of the evidence and information, in just the last 40 years, then evaluating the last 170 years, taken in its TOTALITY it is an absolute truth of life before and after this temporary physical life here on Earth.

There are several reasons why people cannot think of a life before and after this life:

1) THE CLOSED MINDED SKEPTIC: It is good and healthy to be skeptical, but one who is an OPEN MINDED SKEPTIC. It is important to question, challenge, test, show me the evidence, then confirm and reconfirm. To be a CLOSED MINDED SKEPTIC is a sad state of affairs because how is one ever going to learn new things? How is one ever going to grow ? It is a dead end situation. It is a totally lost cause. In addition, being closed minded, one is limited by the narrow mind, and thoughts only within your comfort zone. If your eyes are closed you will never see. If your ears are closed you will never hear. The more you become aware the more you realize how close minded many people truly are.

2) Most people are simply not aware, nor have any knowledge at all, of the massive amount of evidence and information expressed just in the last 40 years proving beyond any shadow of a doubt that there is an afterlife and a very active one. Then you include evidence and information the last 170 years there is simply no doubt, it is not even close. Because the time and effort by people has NOT been made to read this information.

3) Many people have great difficulty thinking outside of their comfort zone. One should NEVER accept anything based on blind faith, blind belief, or trust. For me belief and faith don't mean anything. It is FACTS backed up by impeccable evidence that counts for me.

4) People get trapped by their belief system and never entertain any thoughts outside that system. They become hostage to their own beliefs. So many are prisoners of a specific belief system. People just put on their blinders and see nothing else. They just associate with their own like minded group of people; indeed then they feel safe. It is such a sad situation. Never to entertain different concepts. Any thought that is different is a threat. Everything simply becomes a mental habit.

5) People are a product of their past, culture and upbringing and many times that conditioning carries through the rest of their life. Take for instance, I was raised in an Italian Family in the Bronx where all faith was placed in the Roman Catholic Church. There never was questioning, or to ask does this make any sense? Just an acceptance of the doctrines of the church. That was it. I never noticed any glimmer to question, just blind acceptance.

6) For many, things must be kept simple. If concepts get too complicated that could pose a problem. Most of the organized religions of the world keep things simple, in which you are born, you die, you are here once and there is heaven, hell, punishment and the devil and by the way send me your money.

7) Often people simply want to be told what to believe. Why let somebody else tell you what to think? It simply could be an expression of being lazy.

8) With people there can be such a great fear of death that they will grab on to any faith or belief that gives them hope.

9) Death makes people uncomfortable and there is an attitude of ONLY NOW. What most don't realize, "so called death" is the beginning of a whole new life. It is just the transition to the next plane of life. It is the transfer from one dimension to the next. The tunnel is the path to the next dimension, which is practically right on top of us.

10) People rely on their crude five senses to perceive reality. If a person cannot detect something with their five senses then it cannot exist. If you cannot detect something it does not mean it does not exist! An analogy that is used often is the "dog whistle." The frequency is so high that humans cannot hear it but dogs can hear it!

11) There is great Media bias, prejudice, arrogance and "a know it all attitude" of preconceived ignorance, without ever carefully examining the massive volumes of evidence just in the last 40 years. Many times The Media portrays a world of distortions, half-truths, false narratives and misrepresentation, or just simply outright lies! I say, stop lying and look at the totality of the evidence! Everything connected to the so-called "Paranormal" has to be ghost hunting and demons, monsters lurking in the shadows. THIS IS NOT A GHOST STORY. Ghosts are spirits who for various reasons, trauma, such as murder or don't realize they have died, get stuck here in the physical plane of Earth. They "hang around" the Earth plane. Ghosts have not moved on yet; being still Earthbound after "death." They have not traveled to the Spirit World, Astral planes, where they belong. Ghosts are harmless souls not like Hollywood makes them out to be. Ghosts are uncommon but they do occur. Spirit people visit us from the Spirit World also called the Astral realm.

As I have explained previously I'm an evidence guy, show me the evidence and it better be impeccable, beyond any reproach. Remember I was the ultimate skeptic, the kid from the Bronx who became the medicine and science guy. I am not interested in belief or faith. It works for many, but not for me. In many respects I feel sorry for people that base things on faith or belief and NOT on evidence and facts.

If one examines all the evidence the last 170 years or even better just the last 40 years looking at the TOTALITY of evidence from the NDE, the ADC, the DBV, the EVP fields then you add the Reincarnation and the Life between Lives (LBL) clinical evidence you end up with "mountains" of evidence and the ONLY rational inescapable fact is that there is a life before and after this one and the Afterlife is very active here in this Earth School. In fact, it is so compelling; it is irrational not to realize there is an Afterlife after looking at the totality of all this information and evidence. The problem is people do not take the time and effort to read these volumes of information and evidence. It is all there. You just have to read it. Many times people want to be "spoon fed." There are no shortcuts. If you have the burning desire inside of you there is an immense amount of reading ahead, but it sure is worth it!

Extremely important is the following:

NO ONE, I MEAN NO ONE, HAS EVER COME CLOSE TO DISPROVING THE TOTALITY OF ALL THIS EVIDENCE OF A LIFE BEFORE AND AFTER THIS ONE. NEVER EVER!!!

All the time the conversation goes something like this, "Have you read and examined the volumes of evidence from all the NDE, ADC, EVP, DBV, Reincarnation and LBL's, plus several other fields?" The answer invariably is NO. So then what do you base your rejection of the Afterlife on, if you have not seen all the massive volumes of evidence and information that can fill up many vast rooms? The skeptic has no answer, but a feeling of preconceived ignorance, a totally closed mind. They have a feeling, which means nothing! 'Feelings' are not evidence and facts!

When you analyze the evidence just the last 40 years and compare it to your feelings or a non-existent argument, the skeptic finds themselves in a pathetic, pitiful situation.

There will always be people who will not accept these truths of a life before and after this one, no matter what evidence is shown since they are devoid of rational thought. There will always be people who are not capable of rational, objective, analytical thought. To be very blunt you cannot enlighten stupid, ignorance or arrogance. There is overwhelming proof we come into this life from the same place and return to the same place when this life here ends. The beautiful thing is we don't have to rely on hope, faith or belief; we now know as fact backed up by vast amounts of impeccable evidence.

Now let us briefly talk about the medical and scientific communities. Since I was a member of these communities all of my professional life, I know this well. I like to call it "Egos and Fiefdoms." First, dates may change, names my change and locations but human nature never changes. There have been countless physicians and scientists in all kinds of specialties who have heavily contributed to all these fields of NDE, ADC, EVP, DBV, Reincarnation, and LBL for a very long time. Some of these individuals are the best minds in the world. Many of these professionals started out to disprove the Afterlife and it turned out they proved it instead, many times over. As I mentioned no one has ever disproved the existence of an Afterlife, EVER!!!.

Like many professions; you have lots of egos with private agendas. Maintaining the Fiefdom is the central issue. In medicine and science there are all kinds of inner circles, elite groups who have the power of the purse for money to support research. These groups feed each other and take care of each other. There is much unjustifiable self-importance, corruption, and cronyism. One had better follow the line with the group mind set. If one does research on many of these Afterlife disciplines, they will be ignored; if not then attacked with no basis for the attack. Many times intimidation will be used. Although, very rigorous experimental methods were used, these groups are uncomfortable with the conclusions of the existence of the Afterlife.

In science and medicine a true investigator ALWAYS FOLLOWS THE EVIDENCE, NO MATTER WHERE IT LEADS AND WHAT IT SAYS! I say how dare a person become uncomfortable with the evidence since it does not fit their preconceived ideas, prejudice or ignorance. The truth does not care about one being uncomfortable. The truth will always succeed over time. The truth is there and a time will come when it prevails. The idea of truth, its time has come.

No conversation would ever be complete unless we talk about THE SKEPTICS OF HISTORY. There are countless examples in history of proof of the closed minded, arrogant, ignorant and misinformed position by The Skeptic. The following is a few examples:

1) The Wright Brothers and flying were laughed at in the beginning.
2) The Bell Telephone, met resistance, as being ridiculous.
3) Darwin's theory of evolution was laughed at and met with contempt.
4) Pasteur's concept that germs cause disease was considered fiction.
5) Edison's idea of the light bulb was considered idiotic.
6) Sending rockets into space was considered not practical.
7) Even Penicillin was NOT accepted for quite awhile by the medical establishment.

There are many more examples but you get the idea. If things were left to the skeptics we would still be in caves trying to light a fire! We just have to wait for this generation of skeptics to die off then the following generations will accept life, before and after this life, as natural.

Now let us talk briefly about the organized religions of the world. Some religions today discuss the cycle of the soul or Reincarnation. However, most religions today do not. When Christianity in 313 AD became a recognized religion in the Roman Empire by the conversion of the Roman Emperor Constantine, all references to Reincarnation were removed from the Holy Scriptures. The Romans were worried if the people realized they were eternal and could return, control of the populace could be lost. The Romans were all about control of the people. It was politics, plain and simple. Then further, at the Council of Nicea in 325 AD, the tenets of the theology of Christianity were solidified with no basic changes through the numerous centuries. "Egos and Fiefdoms": to maintain power, control of the flock, their status, position, and money.

Now if one thinks of today, has it changed much among the "religious power brokers" of the organized religions of the world? I think not. The methods may not be as direct or brutal as in the Roman days but it still is about the control of "The Flock" whether it is through self-perpetuating guilt and some form of punishment and reward if you listen to what they say about The Other Side. Many religions never want you to question anything; what they want is a "herd of sheep," which leads to total ignorance.

Human nature never changes. RELIGIONS ARE A MAN MADE EXPERIENCE! To actually think the truth of Source or God, can be confined and defined by humans, defies all logic. All these religions claim they have the truth, and if you are not part of their religion you are missing the truth about The Other Side. EVERY CHURCH CLAIMS THEY ARE THE TRUE CHURCH! Furthermore, if you don't follow the rules of the church, punishment is waiting for you in The Spirit World. Now we have been taught we have an all loving, unconditional loving God. Punishment is waiting for us on The Other Side. Now does that make any sense? Fear fills up churches but love does not. Plus, there is extensive information on the distortions of the Holy Scriptures the last two thousand plus years. It is like a person tells a secret to another person by the time that secret gets to the 20th person it has no resemblance to the original secret from the first person.

Something should be briefly mentioned about those who see demons behind every tree and under every bush. If you examine from numerous sources, especially Newton's compendium of works and several others there is no hell, no demons, and no retribution waiting for us when we return Home to The Spirit World. Numerous sources have indicated this. The demons, hell and punishment come right out of medieval belief systems. It is based on fear, superstition and has ruined countless lives through the numerous centuries. The only place souls truly suffer is here on Earth where there is evil. The Spirit World is composed of endless unconditional love, kindness, forgiveness, compassion, gratitude and patience; it is NOT a place of punishment, terror and fear.

The problem basically being if any idea does not agree with the tenets of a particular organized religion, immediately the reflex non thinking response is that it is the devil. This is their "fall back" position. Not only is this total nonsense but quite childish. The devil and Hell is simply a fear tactic for control. However, remember organized religions do not want thinking adults which they cannot control, who challenge. They want children who are easily controlled. Why would anyone want a religion to do their thinking for them?

There is a great truth that has circulated a long time through numerous sources and that is whether you believe in a doctrine, dogma, a creed or any kind of religious belief; EVERYONE will after the transition called death LIVE. The reason being it is an unalterable law in this universe. IT HAS NOTHING TO DO WITH MAN MADE RELIGION.

When one examines the massive amount of evidence and information related to The Other Side with all the NDE, ADC, DBV etc. one popular criticism by the skeptic is people are hallucinating due to oxygen deprivation to the brain. Now if one looks at the total big picture from all the information and evidence by countless patients and their physicians, nurses, other medical staff, from just about every discipline in medicine the number of people involved just the last 40 years would fill up many large football stadiums. Now have all these people had their brains deprived of oxygen without them being aware and no complaints? Plus, all these people filling up many large football stadiums are of course all hallucinating! WOW, I think the Skeptics should tell all these people that their brains are all lacking oxygen and are hallucinating.

One has to think about all those people who are NOT sick in any way but witness the DBV with the patient; in addition, all those people, NOT sick who are bystanders who experience the SHARED NDE with the patient, getting a tour of The Other Side too! Then the actual Materializations of "so called" deceased people observed by countless very credible people. The arguments of the skeptics are so pathetically thin. Many times what happens is the skeptics resort to "Name Calling," as a sign of desperation in the debate. "Name Calling" means absolutely NOTHING and accomplishes NOTHING!

Let me add one thing about the courageous men and women in these numerous fields of NDE, ADC, DBV, EVP, OBE, Reincarnation, LBL and many more. These many Mediums within several specialties, physicians and scientists in just about every discipline in medicine and science, and other professionals are courageous people who deserve our ultimate respect and admiration. These people are devoted, dedicated to the cause of communicating and teaching people about the Spirit World, The Other Side, in which we are all part of. These people must be admired since numerous times they are attacked, encounter attempts of intimidation, risk at times personal and professional advancement and financial jeopardy by the mindless skeptics. Of course in any field or profession you will always have charlatans or quacks. I have the utmost respect and admiration for all these courageous people, who we owe a great debt to. And who humanity owes a great debt to. After carefully examining the totality of the massive evidence one has to be a total irrational, ignorant, imbecile not to realize that there is a life before and after this present one and very active indeed.

The bottom line is the Skeptic is the one with the problem not the countless people involved who have proven beyond any rational, reasonable doubt that there is a life before and after this life and very active if one looks. There is an immense amount of evidence and information rigorously obtained that we are eternal spirit beings and yet there is no credible rebuttal. In analysis, I think the biggest problem is people are simply not aware of what has been written about life before and after this life. IT IS ALL THERE, YOU JUST HAVE TO LOOK! There is so much evidence; there is no need to hope anymore within our hearts of a life after this life. It is a fact! There will come a time when daily electronic communication by various methods with the next dimension will be common for all.

CHAPTER 21

LOVE OF THE HEART

This is the most important chapter of the book. This is why we wrote this book. It would have been impossible for me to write this book without my Klea. Her intense eternal love was the driving force behind writing this book. This is a story about an eternal love between a man and a woman that has transcended across dimensions for many millennia. Through the eons of time. The woman is in the higher energy dimension(s) or the Astral realm and the man is here in this basic physical plane called Earth.

The Veil separating this woman and man will never stop the great intense love between them. Love will always overcome the barrier called the Veil, which is simply just a difference in energy frequency vibrations. This eternal couple will always find ways to reach each other and connect. These Twin Souls or Twin Flames will always be together for eternity. I have learned so much from Klea during this Spiritual Journey. I could never thank Source enough for giving me Klea as an eternal blessing and gift. God also gave us the gift of powerful Clairsentience, which occurs but is considered rare. "And the two shall become one." A man could not wish for anything more than a woman like Klea. One can never be separated. In this book my girl and I can only describe to you the truth within our heart of hearts.

The heart is so much more than pumping life giving blood to the body. The heart is for truth, knowing and most of all love. One must be aware of their heart consciousness. The knowing of the heart, which the head will never understand or discern. It is the inner knowing and voices of the heart that guides. The heart is an organ of fire. The heart has the strongest electromagnetic field of the body, even greater than the brain. The heart transmits all kinds of physiological and electromagnetic information to the brain and the rest of the body. The heart has its own mind. This large heart electromagnetic field actually transmits an individual's moods into the surrounding environment; positive emotions such as love, joy, gratitude, compassion, forgiveness but also negative ones of anger, fear, and sadness. The size of the heart electromagnetic field is a direct result of emotions; the negative ones restrict the heart field and the positive emotions expand the field. The heart is a great emotional communicator for the body. A person needs both the logic and analysis of the head but also the love and communication of the heart both working together.

Love, compassion and forgiveness appear to be a universal law of the universe. Love gives all meaning and understanding to our existence. Love is the wheelwork of nature. Love dominates energy transfer in the universe and why we select a specific life. Without love we all would be just an empty shell. Love defines our existence. Love is your way of being, of existing. Love rejuvenates the soul. Anger, hatred, and all forms of negativity eats at the soul.

We can have all the material achievements in this life; money, a fancy lifestyle of the rich and famous, but if it is devoid of love, you have NOTHING. Real love of the heart is priceless beyond any description of words. Words, language is so inadequate to describe love of the heart. People have an unconscious search for feeling loved. We all seek love. When one does not feel loved many will substitute materialistic things in this life. People will be chasing fame, money, power and are still empty and filled with unhappiness because they don't have love in their life. However, it is all a poor substitute for unconditional love. Without love, there is a huge hole in the heart, total emptiness. Absolutely, the only thing that matters is love. Love is the most powerful energy in this spiritual universe; it will transcend dimensions across time and space. For

Source or God his unconditional love created all that is. Souls have been called "sparks of the Divine." It is our hope that Klea and Ura will make a difference in this world with our love. We say to you the reader breathe in the life force of love. Love is not something outside of you, it is within you. Klea and Ura hope this book gives you comfort. Turn up the light within you. That light is love. Love and consciousness never end, they are eternal. Love and consciousness will always find a way.

I wish I could transfer my consciousness to you, the reader, of what I now know and learned and have experienced from this Spiritual Journey. Consciousness is the awareness of everything in the internal and external worlds, dimensions, realities of all creations from Source. Love is important for the expression of consciousness. Love is a driving force of consciousness. If there were no love in this spiritual universe what would be the effect on consciousness? What would consciousness look like then?

The primary purpose of this basic physical realm we call Earth School is the intense experience for the soul to experience all the different manifestations of love, compassion, self sacrifice and yes, the learning from pain. At times, the greatest lessons we learn involve pain. However, how can the soul have compassion and self-sacrifice without love? These qualities all feed from love. The soul is love. The soul is the true essence of a person. The soul is an aspect of consciousness. The soul is consciousness. It is the awakening and integration of the power of love in this physical realm. The connecting force of all souls in this universe is love. There are no limits, no boundaries where your soul and love can lead you.

Klea and Ura have been together for many thousands of years into the Stone Age. The inception of our souls occurred sometime during the Stone Age. This Spiritual Journey has had many unexpected twists and turns of experiences and revelations. Reincarnation simply means the soul returns to this Earth School in a new body after death. This process of death and Reincarnation, souls experience numerous times, this roundtrip from the spiritual world to Earth and other worlds. Reincarnation has been described as a window into eternity. As one examines Klea and Ura's Reincarnation Chart, one sees our numerous past lives across ethnic groups, race and nationalities, which we are all connected to the ultimate matrix of consciousness of all souls. The Reincarnation Chart will never be complete until I, Ura Cross the Veil and return Home. Remember that is just some of the lives shared by my girl and I. It does not include the past lives we were apart or not as a couple.

Klea and Ura are Twin Souls or Twin Flames. In the universe, each person is created as a duality, both male and female. Twin Souls are from their inception in time a pair that was created. They are two halves of the perfect whole. Everyone has another half. What can affect one part of the pair the other is affected. When one part of the Twin Flame is in pain the other will also express it. Twin Souls can never be separated for all eternity. It is a bond that can never be severed.

Our love was forged over many thousands of years, over 17,000 years, across numerous life times across time and space. Long ago our souls mated as one. It is an unbreakable love. It is an unshakable love. It is a real eternal relationship. A bond that transcends dimensions, time, and past lives. There is a great will to connect. The power of the will of love. Our spiritual connection by Clairsentience, Clairvoyance and Clairaudience is just as real as flesh and blood. My Klea is still an integral, active part of my life. We are still together. We have a real relationship. She is always close to my consciousness and heart. In many respects she is closer to my mind and heart than when she was here in this basic physical realm. As described numerous times in the text, her energy power of Clairsentience is an overwhelming expression of her love. No language can ever describe these feelings.

The soul is the spirit, enduring part and essence of a person. The soul does not die and continues for millennia to infinity. The soul is the part of you that makes you who you are and that will live on after your "so called death." Death is just a process of you awakening to your immortal self and returning HOME. We now know at the time of Crossing the Veil or returning HOME, our Etheric Soul Body, which is a mirror image of the dead physical body, rises up and out. It has been described countless times, the next dimension of life is even more real than the one we just left. It is about never again being afraid to die. There is no such thing as death. Our spirit is alive and always will be. We are as eternal as Source, who created us.

Since the beginning of time there have been attempts to define love. In my viewpoint, love is a supernova of energy within the soul that has matching energy vibration frequencies with other souls. It is a matching of energy vibration frequencies within souls. Analogous to a quickening of matching energy frequencies related to all the different types of love and communication.

When I started this book, I mentioned that this book was written for the reader, to make them aware of The Other Side or The Spirit World, which is the true reality and the power and wonder of love across dimensions of time and space. To make the reader realize it is all about love. To those readers who truly understand love, it is your story too. This is a book about and for you. It has been a great happiness and joy for Klea and Ura to take you, the reader, on this Spiritual Journey of love with us. Love transcends dimensions. Klea and Ura know that love can change the world here. We are so much more than flesh, we are love. The Veil between The Other Side and This Side is thinning. The differences of the energy vibration frequencies are starting to diminish between these two dimensions. People are becoming aware of asking the questions: Where did I come from? Why am I here? What is the meaning or purpose of life? Where do I return to? People need to understand their power, to embrace it. To realize how magnificent they are as eternal Interdimensional Spirit Beings (ISB). Once you know the truth it is empowering and liberating.

This Spiritual Journey of love between Klea and Ura began long ago and has no ending because love has no ending in this spiritual universe. Since love never dies; it is forever. Love always lives on.

CHAPTER 22

THE ETERNAL NEVER ENDING LOVE STORY

As I write this now more information is coming to me from The Other Side and from my Klea. This story has no ending. I thought the previous chapter of Love of the Heart was going to be the last chapter. However, every few days something significant happens between my girl and I, or some revelation becomes available, thus it continues with no end in sight; which is great because this is a joyful awakening of love and knowing.

Information is passed between my Klea and I in three different settings, our morning meditations and visits that usually take place on the living room couch. At night meditations and visits at the dining room table or on the living room couch and in bed having our interdimensional pillow talk.

Lately, however, we just sit together in the recliner chair in the family room about 10:00 PM in the evenings and just BE. At times it is good just TO BE. Just being silent is a connection for us too. I will talk about the recliner chair a little bit later.

As I previously mentioned to her I said we had many kids through the ages in our pillow talk. We both laughed. The next morning she told me a total of 38 children. Now as an afterthought I never thought of adding up the children in The Reincarnation Chart. As I previously mentioned sometimes I can be dense. So weeks later I did. If you add them up and you subtract the one stillborn birth in the past life in 703 AD Lithuania with Myrath and Raj where we had four children, three daughters and one son and not counting the present day two sons you come up with exactly 38 total children in our past lives. We also laughed in bed of all the weddings we had through the many past lives, again and again. It was a repeating grand old time. At one point my Klea told me there are between 200-300 people waiting for me and to greet me and to welcome me HOME on The Other Side when I Cross the Veil. Klea also told me that I would see all my children again from past lives. Remember these people will be loved ones and friends from all our past lives including the present one.

Now there are concepts one needs to understand about The Other Side. There are volumes of information that would fill up vast rooms about The Hall Of Records and Our Life Charts. The Hall of Records is like a vast Library beyond our comprehension that has everything in this spiritual universe of infinity that existed: memories, thoughts, actions, emotions, deeds, words, moments, everything! Everything related to the total matrix of consciousness in the universe. In the Hall of Records every soul has what they call Life Charts. Remember the laws of physics are different in these higher energy dimensions, on The Other Side than here, thus they are not like charts as we think in our realm. These are the records of total information on all the reincarnations of that specific soul. I have asked my Klea several times do you go to the Hall of Records to get information on all our reincarnations together? I always receive a strong Clairsentience yes. I very much look forward to the day when we both can go to the Hall of Records. These records have been called the Akashic Records or The Mind of God. A vast beyond comprehension compendium of all events, thoughts, words, emotions, intent that occurred in the past, present, and future in the infinite universe.

She has told me several times that we were happy in these past lives. What she has told me is the following so far; that we died together in two past lives, one in 1806 AD as Toby and Kenneth as the ship sank in the

Atlantic Ocean and killed in Honduras in 535 AD as Rotta and Tiko. We were very young in life in 1806 however, much older in the one in 535 AD. Furthermore, in two lives we also died very young. The one in 1806 again but also in ancient Egypt in 3016 BC as Mira and Ptolemy. In fact, recently I started to have images, visions of our last moments in the life in Honduras. I could see it was at night and our village was attacked. There were torches, people running and screaming. Tan skinned men with just bottom trunks holding torches and having knives. The reflection of the torches in the night. These images repeated several times and were quite vivid and detailed. I actually could hear the screaming. This was a surprise to me because all these many months I just had visions of three past lives we were together, namely ancient Rome in 207 BC as Antonia and Claudius; 1736 England as Clare and Benjamin and 1806 on a ship at sea as Toby and Kenneth.

Now the subjective Clairvoyance in my mind's eye has been improving in "leaps and bounds." What I have been seeing in our meditations and visits which my Klea confirms by Clairsentience is the following: when I ask her to hold hands with me I now see her placing both hands in mine. With the target Clairsentience when I ask her to touch my heart, I now see her arm reach out and touch my heart. We have ENERGY KISSES all the time where I just receive gentle waves of Clairsentience just on my face, nowhere else. Plus, now I can visualize her coming close to me. ENERGY TOUCHING is just an indescribable experience. Her love is within me, in my very being. Many times now I see her place her arm around me. When we have a meditation session or visit on the living room couch she sits next to me. However, during the sessions in the dining room she stands right in front of me. At the breakfast table she sits in the chair to my right. Since I document everything; often just after a meditation or visit, I send myself an email of what occurred. Many times my girl is actually looking over my shoulder as I am typing on the computer. I ask her if you are looking over my shoulder and she confirms with a Clairsentience yes, just amazing. My girl always knew how to "pick me up" or "cheer me up." Just to make me laugh. For instance, through my Clairvoyance, I see, she will put on Toby's Blue Bonnet Hat from 1806 and smile and laugh. Seeing that image just "cracks me up." She really is something!

When my Klea first got sick with that horrible cancer we purchased a very comfortable leather recliner chair in the family room so she could watch TV in comfort. Who was to know that her last moments here on THIS SIDE would be in that recliner chair? This chair has great meaning for us. There are times now when after we communicate at night on the living room couch I will not go to bed right away but go into the family room and sit in our recliner chair and watch TV. She follows me and sits and cuddles with me. With my Clairvoyance I can see her. Several times I ask her to HUG and I receive a very strong incredible Clairsentience energy pulse in my whole chest area that travels through my complete body down to my fingertips. It is very powerful. You can't miss it!

Our routine does change often. Many mornings I have my cup of coffee in the family room recliner chair and we sit together and about 10:00 PM at night we sit in the chair again. We have been "hanging out" a lot in the recliner chair. I always do my "Alpha Checks" to confirm she is with me but with my improved Clairvoyance I can see her. Every time I ask her to give me a big hug or merge within me I immediately receive such an incredible blast of Clairsentience energy that it is literally overwhelming. It literally goes through my whole body down to my finger tips. WOW! If I wasn't sitting down it would knock me over. It tells me she is not only there with me but she is listening to me, hears me and knows exactly what I am saying. We laugh now about my return HOME and we are reunited on The Other Side, that when we merge our spirits, the Clairsentience love energy will be explosive, something to behold!

When the weather is pleasant we will sit outside on the patio in the backyard. Usually, this will occur after a midday meditation and visit. My Clairvoyance sees her sitting next to me and she always "BLASTS ME" with her Clairsentience as there is no doubt. When she was here in this basic physical realm we always sat outside holding hands.

You see, her energy of love goes through me and HER LOVE IS WITHIN ME! I asked her why her Clairsentience was so powerful in the recliner chair. She told me because she Crossed the Veil in that chair. Lately, we have been spending a lot of time together in the mornings and at night in the recliner chair. In many respects we are closer now than when she was here in this physical plane. I could never thank Source enough for giving me Klea as an eternal blessing and gift throughout these many thousands of years and past life times.

When one reads Dr. Michael Newton's books and several others there is volumes of information regarding our Spirit Guides and the Council of Elders. This massive information base has been around for a very long time. What are these entities? Well, your Spirit Guides are like your eternal "guidance counselors," your best friends. The Spirit Guides have agreed to watch over all your incarnations. Every soul has one major Spirit Guide that never leaves you for all eternity. Then you have others that come and go depending on specific needs. These Spirit Guides can advise, council you and place ideas in your mind but cannot tell you what to do as you experience an incarnation here in Earth School or another world. These Guides are strictly in an advisory capacity. Remember we always have free will. It is one of the laws of the universe. However, your guides have knowledge of every detail about you. At times, I would say your Spirit Guides know you better than you know yourself.

Now my personal Spirit Guides have been in my meditations for quite awhile. I have three men, which I simply call "my guys." I have given them names "Mike, Henry, and Carl." I know exactly what they look like. They kind of sit back and let me do my thing. Maybe, they just feel I have things in hand. I don't know why I have three. Although, I do notice at times they put thoughts or give me messages in my mind when I wake up in the mornings. Lately, "my guys" have been smiling at me. I believe my Master Spirit Guide who never leaves me is the one I call Carl. A tall wise thin man with a beard. We will definitely have to get to know each other better.

Now as I stated at the beginning of this chapter revelations and new information become available all the time. I started using meditations specific for connecting with my Spirit Guides. Well, I have five Spirit Guides. Carl is my Master Spirit Guide, Mike is my guide for when I am interacting with a Medium; so is my Medium Spirit Guide; Henry helps with analytical issues, finances, problem solving. However, I also have two women Spirit Guides: Olivia and Erica. Olivia helps with everything and Erica helps with love relationships. They all step into my energy field (Aura) and we merge energy. The tingling, vibrations, tremors, chills, of energy down my arms and especially my legs are incredible. All souls have their unique energy vibration. My five Spirit Guides have a specific energy vibration when we merge energy. They are all different. When Klea and I merge our energy with Clairsentience it is a totally different feeling. In my regular meditation connections with my guides, I ask questions and there is an immediate Clairaudience response. My Spirit Guides are always with me. We all have Spirit Guides. We are never alone. I see them all through my Clairvoyance and I know what they all look like. I now look forward to getting together with all five of them on a regular basis.

We all have a Council of Elders, this is the most common name, however other titles have been used. These ancient wise masters are a committee that varies in numbers, for example, from three to as many as twelve.

This Council oversees our many lives. Before and after every incarnation you meet with this Council to discuss your progress in detail about the advancement of your soul spirituality. Your Spirit Guide(s) accompanies you to these meetings in the Hall of Justice. What you did right and wrong. What you missed. Did you accomplish your objectives for this incarnation? For instance, say you had to work on compassion or forgiveness more. Essentially, OK soul how did you make out in this last life or incarnation? Even though the Council knows every detail about you. Everything is for the evolutionary benefit, the advancement of the spirituality of your soul. This learning curve of the soul is a very long process. Remember our souls came into existence more than 17,000 years ago. We have now reached the Intermediate level of our soul spirituality. For the Council of Elders their love, patience, compassion and understanding have no limits.

Lately, my Council of Elders have started to reveal themselves to me in my meditations. I have three on my committee, one woman and two men. The woman started to reveal herself first in my meditations or visits with my Klea. She was sitting and had a very kind, gentle, smiling face with great wisdom. Immediately, I sensed she was a friend for all eternity and understood Klea and Ura's intense love as Twin Souls or Twin Flames. I asked my Klea about her and she told me she knows her and her name. Now for some reason in reading the information base from numerous sources the names of these Spirit Guides, Council of Elders and the eternal names of other souls can be very difficult to pronounce and are quite unusual in spelling at times.

My Klea told me she knows the two men and also their names on my Council. Both of the men on my Council have now made themselves known to me. The first man who revealed himself is a tall smiling handsome man, who I also feel is a friend. The second man and last to make himself known is small, short with black hair and mustache. I feel he is very funny but also a friend for all eternity. All the members of my Council wore robes; and I now know all their names. Now in deep meditation through my Clairvoyance I see them surround me smiling and raise their arms above me. Now my Klea told me twice during our Interdimensional Pillow Talk that her Council of Elders has four members, three women and one man. We will see, in the future, where this all takes us.

There is another concept that has been extensively written about by Newton and others and that is the existence of THE PRESENCE above and behind the Council of Elders in the Hall of Justice. I never gave it much thought. It is like one of those things you read, record, and forget about it and you say to yourself well that's nice and move on; yeah right!

First, what is THE PRESENCE and description? It is an overwhelming feeling, a higher force at The Council Meetings. Numerous people have quotes that: "This is as close to God as we get." More advanced Souls state they don't think THE PRESENCE is God but some deified entity or entities, which has immense capabilities and power vastly superior to The Council of Elders. THE PRESENCE is there to help the Council and the soul. This is a great omnipotent loving energy force in the Spirit World. It is a great pulsating violet, white and silver radiating light above and behind The Council in the Hall of Justice.

Now lately in my meditations and visits with my Klea, everybody is there smiling, my Spirit Guides, my Higher Self, which is the part of my soul energy left behind in the Spirit World, my Council of Elders, and I now see THE PRESENCE. Many times my three Council members are standing, surrounding me and raising their arms above me smiling, which I previously mentioned. At times they are laughing, I guess at what I am saying. I'm considered a funny guy. I now several times in meditations merge my love and energy with the love energy of THE PRESENCE with my talking out loud to THE PRESENCE. Well, the only thing I can say is Holy Shit!!! I see THE PRESENCE radiating violet, silver, white light showering down on me and the power of the energy is OFF THE SCALE. Every time it happens now it blows me away. I cannot even put into words the power of this love energy. It takes my breath away. In meditations I will talk out loud, when I feel the energy of THE PRESENCE, at times I can't even talk! I can see being right there with the Council in the Hall of Justice; the energy, the power can be too much of THE PRESENCE. It is totally different from my Klea's Clairsentience love energy. Several times Klea and I discussed it and she feels it too. I know, wild shit, right, maybe some of you reading this will think I am nuts! However, I only can state the truth within my heart, as rationally, objectively and analytically as humanly possible. I know what I felt and experienced numerous times. One cannot describe it to others; people have to experience it for themselves. Then and only then, they will know and understand. Out of frustration, I previously mentioned, I wish, I could transfer my consciousness to you, the reader, of what I now know, learned and experienced from this Spiritual Journey.

People will never understand it, like the experience of the feelings of Clairsentience. Until they experience it themselves. If they never experience it. They will never know. I understand it because I experience it. I cannot project that understanding to you.

I mentioned briefly about the HIGHER SELF. In every incarnation the soul leaves part of its energy on The Other Side. The degree of soul energy that is left behind differs from soul to soul and incarnation to incarnation. The brain here in human form could never accommodate the full, 100%, of the soul energy. The brain would explode. It simply would be too much energy; it is physics. Related to a compatibility of the dimension one is in; here we only use about 20% of our brain, however once we return HOME we use 100%. There are dramatic increases in brain utilization, memory retention, and consciousness.

There is another very important concept that needs to be explained which there is much information on from many sources. In every incarnation a detailed Life Chart is very carefully devised by you, the soul, your Spirit Guides, Council of Elders and several others, with the intent of outlining the objectives for the next incarnation to improve your soul spirituality. Remember it is all about the evolution of the soul spirituality. This plan goes into great detail in the events of this next life here in Earth School or another world. Realism is always used if the soul can truly accomplish their objectives. As a soul lives this life, the plan can somewhat change because we all have free will. Free will is an unalterable law in this magnificent spiritual universe of an infinity of dimensions.

On The Other Side we have access to the Life Charts we wrote but also access to our loved ones charts as well. Knowing about the creation of this Life Chart the realization occurred to me that prior to this present incarnation we both accepted and agreed on the events of this life. Meaning we both consented and agreed to my beautiful Klea departing from this life with lung cancer at the age of 66. Remember if one looks at the Reincarnation Chart the last time we shared a past life was in 1903 AD in Italy as Angelina and Emilio in the village of Sant'Angelo Di Piove Di Sacco, having a son and a daughter. This realization struck me like a thunderbolt of lightning that we both agreed she would exit with lung cancer. The love was so great that we accepted this. I was astounded by the magnitude of this realization and love. My Klea in our various communications confirmed this. The great desire by Klea and Ura to reincarnate again, knowing how this would end for my girl is overwhelming. The problem being now that I, Ura, for these temporary years is left here in this Earth plane, although still together with Klea, separated by the Veil with all the pain, anguish, and suffering that goes along with it. There is a very big difference when you plan your next incarnation and see it written compared to actually then experience it in this life!

The next question is, as we know every incarnation of a soul has the purpose of learning lessons. All in the ultimate objective of the betterment of the soul on the learning curve. We accelerate our spirituality for God and learn for God; to become closer to God. Source gives us the opportunity to perfect our souls. So what were the lessons in this life for Klea and I? I honestly have no idea. Was it for me to experience the intense pain of losing her so early to appreciate her more? My love for her has no limits nor boundaries so I truly don't understand. When I Cross the Veil I will find out. There will be lots of discussions.

In summary what really does happen when we all go through a cycle of one life. First, there is extensive detailed planning of our next life with our Spirit Guides, The Council of Elders, and other advanced souls. Great time and effort is spent in producing a detailed Life Chart, composed of primary and secondary objectives, lessons, in what the spirit in question needs to learn from this specific incarnation. The spirit comes into this life with their specific Spirit Guides and Angels. The life can change somewhat because we all have free will, a universal law of the universe. Upon completion of this life we return HOME and review, evaluate and discuss how this life was in relation to our lessons or objectives with our Spirit Guides and Council of Elders. Always remember it is all about the advancement of the spirituality of the soul. We then return to our Soul Group. This is a very brief summary of what occurs, although much more happens in between all these steps.

All my life I never gave a thought about the Spirit World, The Other Side, Reincarnation, and everything that goes along with it. Remember I was the ultimate skeptic, the no nonsense, hard nose Bronx boy who entered the fields of medicine and science. It took an awful lot for me to make a change of this magnitude. The tremendous shock of my beautiful girl exiting this life early was a colossal "wake up" call for me, which then started me on this amazing Spiritual Journey. I would have never taken this journey and have written this book, if she did not Cross the Veil. If this is true, what an astronomical price to pay to get my attention.

There is something else too, in my life I have had six instances where I survived unscathed under ridiculous circumstances pertaining to auto crashes and very serious illness in which I walked away perfectly fine; as if nothing happened. My Guardian Angels were certainly working overtime. Was I protected all my life for the destiny of traveling on this Spiritual Journey; with the intent to teach others about The Other Side? Is that my mission in this incarnation to give an understanding and teaching to others about the Spirit World? When I asked this question to my Klea, she gave me a very strong Clairsentience yes, when we were both in the recliner chair one night. Related to this a key is the writing of this book for everyone, for the man and woman on the street so they can understand about the Spirit World, The Other Side. I will find out when I return HOME, across the Veil. Well, I don't have to wait now, in all my meditations and visits lately with my Klea, and everyone else, Council of Elders, Spirit Guides, I have been told several times that writing this book is in my Life Chart. It would have been impossible for me to write this book without my Klea. We advanced so far because of Klea. Her great desire to connect with powerful love was the key. There are many more questions than answers.

Two things started to happen, I was constantly seeing 1010 on all kinds of clocks and I started to notice with my Clairvoyance that there were several angels around me. Now about the spiritual meaning of the numbers 1010. According to my research I have a spiritual team supporting me and I am awakening to my spiritual self. Well, that certainly is true regarding the Spiritual Journey of love I have been on for quite awhile with my Klea.

I started to notice through my Clairvoyance that several angels were surrounding me. I first noticed them a number of times around me in the family room. Then again when I was at the grocery store standing in line and other times too. I did not give it much thought especially after all the revelations we have experienced in this long Spiritual Journey. However, I decided to ask my girl in our daily meditations about these angels. I asked her a number of times and she strongly confirmed this with a Clairsentience yes, that I have angels around me. Furthermore, I have a total of five angels around me for protection. This was confirmed many times. Now obviously I asked why are these angels around me? Does it have to do with my mission before I Cross the Veil and return HOME of teaching others about the Spirit World? Klea confirmed this several times that I am protected by the angels to allow me to complete my mission of teaching people here in Earth School about The Other Side, the Spirit World.

I know one thing whenever I see an ornament of an angel on a Christmas Tree it has a totally different meaning for me now. Angels are not ornaments in our imagination but the "real deal." There are several different types of angels depending on their purpose. Angels are the guardians from Source in the universe. As the Holy Spirit is pure direct love energy from Source.

As I began this book describing our Spiritual Journey of eternal love of Klea and Ura, I stated that this story has no ending. This was our Spiritual Journey. Everyone has to find their own spiritual path, their own journey. I want to thank Klea for always being there for me, as she waits for me when I Cross the Veil. Once again our love will be whole again when I Cross the Veil. It is all about finishing this book then returning HOME to her. There are no limits to my love for her. Twin Flames or Twin Souls can never be denied of being together. Who knows what new revelations will surface in the future. We are in this world but not of it. When we are born into this world we inhale, when we depart from this world we exhale to go HOME. When my time comes to Cross the Veil and return HOME, my Klea will be waiting for me and will take my hand and take me HOME for all eternity. My beautiful Klea has told me several times she is preparing a home for us, Our Home. She will bring me HOME. We will save the best for last. We will always watch over our loved ones. We are protectors. I will exercise one of the laws of the universe and that is the law of free will; THIS WILL BE MY LAST INCARNATION! 62 incarnations is enough. I am done. This will be my last returning trip to the next dimension of life, The Other Side. I am staying there now; not coming back, enough is simply enough!

I could never thank Source enough for giving me Klea as a true blessing and gift for all eternity. We could never thank God enough for giving Klea and Ura the gift of Clairsentience that binds our souls forever. I think our wedding invitation in 1977 said it best "The miracle of love is that love is given to us to give to one another." On our monument at the cemetery it reads "And The Two Shall Become One".

I only know one thing that it is absolute that love has been given to all of us, immortal souls, as a blessing and gift from Source for all eternity. The highest and most sacred energy vibration in this universe is love. There is nothing but God in all of us for eternity and infinity. We are all ONE with God and love.

Appendix A – Key Definitions and Abbreviations

THE OTHER SIDE	The Spirit World; the higher vibration energy dimension practically right on top of our earth plane
NDE	Near Death Experience
ADC	After Death Communication
DBV	Deathbed Visions
OBE	Out-of-Body Experience
EVP	Electronic Voice Phenomena: Recording of Spirit People Voices
REINCARNATION	The Rebirth of a Soul in a New Body
LBL	Life between Lives in the Spirit World
CLAIRSENTIENCE	The Feeling of Spirit Energy
CLAIRAUDIENCE	The Hearing or Listening for Spirit Voices
CLAIRVOYANCE	To See Spirit and Images
TWIN SOULS or TWIN FLAMES	At Creation a Female and Male Souls as a Duality
EMDR	Eye Movement Desensitization Reprocessing
ISB	Interdimensional Spirit Beings; Who and What We Are

Appendix B – The Reincarnation Chart

PRESENT	Felecia and Leonard – **New York, USA** – two sons
1903 AD	**Italy,** Angelina and Emilio – lived in the village of Sant'Angelo di Piove di Sacco – two children – one son and one daughter
1806 AD	**Ship at sea** (Atlantic Ocean) - Toby and Kenneth, on route from Ireland to America....Just married, we were so young, no children.....Perished at sea
1736 AD	**England** – Clare and Benjamin – had one child...a daughter
1642 AD	**Germany** – Safha and Tandel – had three children – three daughters
1541 AD	**Spain** – (The Renaissance) – Ana and Franco – had two children – one son and one daughter
703 AD	**Lithuania** (before it was Lithuania) Myrath and Raj – had five children – one still born – three daughters and one son
535 AD	**Honduras** (before it was called Honduras, in Central America) – Rotta and Tiko – had five children – four sons and one daughter
135 AD	**Mesopotamia –** Atta and Vebra – had three sons – Mesopotamia was an ancient region in the Eastern Mediterranean Sea, bordered by the Zagros Mountains in the northeast, composed of mostly present day Iraq, but also Turkey, Iran, and Syria
207 BC	**Rome, Italy** - Antonia and Claudius – two children – one son and one daughter
1038 BC	**Crimean Peninsula** in the Black Sea (Ukraine, before the name Crimea) – Tika and Noak had six children – three sons and three daughters
3016 BC	**Ancient Egypt –** Mira and Ptolemy – had four children – three sons and one daughter
5050 BC	**Samara Civilization (5th Millennium BC, Upper Volga River, Russia) –** Ena and Farouk – six children – four daughters and two sons

Three Past Lives In The Stone Age

7543 BC	Neolithic Period or New Stone Age
10009 BC	Cusp of the Paleolithic, Old Stone Age and Mesolithic, Middle Stone Age
15043 BC	The Old Stone Age, our first life together here

❦ NOTES

❦ NOTES

❦ NOTES

❦ NOTES

Made in the USA
Middletown, DE
14 August 2020